WASH EACH OTHER'S FEET

HEALING OUR SPIRIT WITH RELATIONAL MINISTRY

By the collaborative efforts of Tammy Amosson
and Fr. Gale White

authorHOUSE™

1663 LIBERTY DRIVE, SUITE 200
BLOOMINGTON, INDIANA 47403
(800) 839-8640
WWW.AUTHORHOUSE.COM

First published by AuthorHouse 09/28/05

ISBN: 1-4208-6520-X (sc)

Printed in the United States of America
Bloomington, Indiana

This book is printed on acid-free paper.

Dedication

We dedicate this book to you- the reader, for whom we prayerfully wrote this. Our hope is that through your own relational ministry journey, you are able to see others through a greater lens of love and in doing so, are able to live more fully in all of your relationships.

To our friends—we thank you for supporting us with your constant prayer, encouragement and unconditional love. We could not have written this book without you.

(From Tammy)
To My husband Brett, my greatest God deal, and to our four miracles; Joshua, Jacob, Luke and baby #4 coming soon! To my parents who were my first relationship teachers and my big sister Kim, who was my first mentor. To Team Amosson, I could not have married into a more awesome family. Thank you for taking me in and loving me as your own. A special thanks to all who helped us watch, baby-sit and raise the Amosson boys. You are our saints!

(From Fr. Gale)
To my adopted daughter, Eileen, and her husband, Dan, thanks for providing me with a home and a family in my retirement years! To my brothers and sisters, thanks for supporting and loving me always. To all of you who I have had the privilege of knowing and the blessing of

sharing our journey together over the years, thank you. Thank you for being part of my experience, life and teaching me about relationships; especially all you engaged and married couples. Keep choosing love; it is the best decision you will make.

To our friend and talented artist Susan Annand, whose amazing artwork adorns our cover; To April LeVay, and all our friends at AuthorHouse who helped us in the publishing process, and to Angela Kalsh our awesome editor.

And most importantly to God – the love of our lives. Thank you for letting two broken disciples carry your message. It is only by your grace that this is possible - Who are we but your humble servants? It is all through you. We love you!

In Loving Memory

Mike Yaconelli holds a very special place in our hearts and in this book. Mike was going to write the prologue for this book prior to a car accident that took him home to be with Jesus in October of 2002. Mike continues to be a great inspiration for us, and his legacy will forever be alive in our heart and soul. To you brother Mike, you modeled how to live authentic love relationships. Thank you for showing us that it is possible. We will keep striving- pray for us!

Contents

PROLOGUE

"In the book of life, the answers aren't in the back."
-Charlie Brown by Charles Schulz

"I can do all things through Christ who strengthens me."
-Phil 4:13

"You shall love the Lord your God . . . You shall love your neighbor as yourself. There is no other commandment greater than these."
-Mk 12:31

Neither of us has ever written a book. The fact that we are doing so now- together is all a "God Deal"! When I talked to Fr. Gale about the idea that God had been putting in my heart and head for sometime he told me that he had something he had to tell me when we next met. When we got together he said he had always told people that I was going to write his book. I was in disbelief as he told me. Certainly he was confusing me with someone else. When we had first met, I was a youth minister and he the Family Life Director.

Why did he think of me? It continues to be a question neither he nor I can answer, but we know that this project was inspired by someone much greater than the two of us. It has been a journey and one that has taught us much, especially about relationships. Everything we talk about in this book has been real in our lives and much of it still current. This is a journey, not a how to book, in as much as an encouragement of hope. We do pray you embrace what God places on your heart through these pages as it was he who inspired it. Only God could bring together a kick boxer, mom to four, youth minister and a motorcycle, truck driving, retired priest!

We wrote this book because we believe the power of God's love manifests itself through relationships. We believe we can know Him more intimately by loving each other, and we believe in you!

(Tammy shares)

"During the course of writing this book, we discovered we were pregnant (I am old so I feel like Elizabeth). We then found out our family was moving. We have never moved, so quite a roller coaster of emotions ensued. A big part of change for a parent is how well your children respond and adapt. We would have to handle this delicately. Our first born son, Joshua, was fine with the move, but had one request. "Please, can I have my own room? Luke talks incessantly and I can't sleep." That was a reasonable request and if it helped him with the transition, we would grant that. Our middle son, Jac, is the easy going one. He is happy wherever he is and as long as there are people nearby that he can hug, he is great. That too will be easy to grant. The youngest child, Luke, was the one we were unsure of. How would his sensitive spirit handle such a change? As I delicately tried to articulate what was happening, Luke simply looked at me and said, "Mom, are you going?" I of course smiled at his question and assured him, "Yes, Luke, I will be going." Now a huge smile of joy beamed across his face and he confidently stated, "Well then I am going too!" I reflected on the trust and simplicity he experienced in the security that his parent would be there. Thus he knew he would be taken care of, he felt secure. I turned to prayer and decided I needed to have the same conversation with my parent, My Father. "God, are you going to be there?" I asked. "Yes, my child, I will always be wherever you are, I am always with you." I now felt the same security I learned from Luke, "Okay God then I will go too, I will go where you lead me Lord, and trust in you."

(Fr. Gale Shares)

"My journey continues to evolve. I have embarked on yet a new ministry in my retirement years. I am currently driving across the country transporting trucks for my beloved brother. I see this as a wonderful opportunity to commune with the countryside, my fellow brethren on the road, and the beauty in nature. I listen to books on tape and take in the refreshing peace and tranquility of God's county. I continue to journey into unfamiliar territory, risking the unknown, and forever challenging myself with new growth opportunities. Many wonder why? "You don't have to do this; they banter, you are retired for goodness sakes." I lovingly respond, I don't' have to do this, I choose to, and I am helping someone I care deeply for, that is enough for me."

We are all challenged to stretch and grow throughout our own spiritual journey. By following the path to Relational Ministry we can grow stronger together!

Introduction:

Wash Each Other's Feet

"If, therefore, I, the master and teacher, have washed your feet, you out to wash each other's feet. I have given you a model to follow, so that as I have done for you should also do."
-Jn 13: 3-5, 13-15

"The world today is hungry for love."
-Mother Teresa

"When he saw him, he had compassion, and went to him and bound up his wounds."
-Lk 10:33-34

*S*usan, a mom of two beautiful daughters, faithfully took her girls to the pool every Friday during the summer for what their family called "Fun Friday". There were some days Susan dreaded the monumental task of packing the kids lotion, goggles, drinks, snacks, towels, dry clothes etc., but the kids loved it and their persistent begging always won out. One "Fun Friday", Susan's girls were having a great time in the community pool, when Susan's attention was drawn to a woman entering the gate. Susan watched as the woman managed to carry her frail teenage daughter in her arms while two toddlers tugged at her legs simultaneously.

Susan was mesmerized, and therefore did not respond fast enough to help the woman. Soon the woman settled in and took her daughter over to a shallow embankment where the water was able to splash playfully over her legs.

As the morning went on, Susan watched her own two daughters throwing a ball back and forth. Suddenly, the overthrown ball whipped past the girls and rolled right next to the girl on the embankment who had been carried in by her mom earlier. Susan was ready to act this time and jumped up ran over to the girl and apologized. The girl giggled and threw the ball back toward the young girls playing. Susan then heard a voice behind her say, "Don't worry she enjoys the activity." Susan turned to find the graceful mom who had carried the girl in earlier. "Hi, I'm Connie," she said with a friendly smile, "and this is Grace." Susan introduced herself and the moms started to visit. Susan thought about how much effort it must have taken for this mom to bring her family to the pool and she reflected on how her own stress earlier paled in comparison. Susan turned to Connie and said, "I saw *you come in earlier and I had wanted to help you, but by the time it registered, you had it all handled. I'm sorry I wasn't of more help. I watched you in amazement." Connie smiled empathetically and said, "Susan, you are sweet. I am use to this, don't give it another thought. You should have seen me trying to carry Grace through the Grand Canyon. Now, I could have really used your help then!" And the two women laughed.*

Susan asked if Connie minded talking about Grace. Connie told her she loved talking about her precious daughter. Connie began by explaining that Grace had a disease that left her severely crippled. One thing she loved more than anything was coming to the pool. Susan looked over at Grace sitting on the embankment and noticed her two siblings nearby playing with her. Susan asked what it was that Grace liked most about coming.

Connie admitted that for a long time she wasn't sure since she can't swim or get fully emerged in the water. Then one day Grace was drawing a picture and it was clearly this community pool. She drew her feet in the way they were right now, cascading off the embankment with the water playfully lapping over them. We realized she likes to come here and place her feet in the water. Perhaps for Grace, it is like swimming.

Susan smiled and told Connie that her favorite gospel story was John 13:14-15 - Jesus washing the disciples' feet. Susan said watching Grace in the water made her think of that image. Connie told Susan that that image was quite fitting. I see her wash the feet of others by influencing their heart. She really is one of God's special angels. Susan could not hold back. Now moved to tears, she told Connie that Grace was not the only one sent to wash feet. Connie had done that for her as well. The two parted ways and Susan has not seen Connie or Grace since although she thinks about them daily. Whenever she hears the gospel story of Jesus washing the disciples' feet, she pictures Grace on the embankment splashing love onto everyone around.

"Fully aware that the Father had put everything into his power and that he had come from God and was returning to God, he rose from supper and took off his outer garments. He took a towel and tied it around his waist. Then he poured water into a basin and began to wash the disciples' feet and dry them with the towel around his waist. You call me 'teacher' and 'master', and rightly so, for indeed I am. If, therefore, I, the master and teacher, have washed your feet, you ought to wash each other's feet. I have given you a model to follow, so that as I have done for you should also do." -Jn 13: 3-5, 13-15

This powerful image of Jesus washing the disciples' feet is one that turns power, prestige, and authority upside down and humility, compassion and service right side up.

Jesus modeled humility by extending himself in service to his beloved disciples. This beautiful visual gives us all an example to aspire to. In Relational Ministry, humility overpowers ego. Relational Ministry is a way by which we can extend ourselves to another through selfless love.

Jesus took the disciples flesh in hand, drawing it to him, he touched the dirt ridden calloused feet of each disciple and cleansed them.

Relational Ministry is about kneeling down before another in humility and in service. There is no place for pride or arrogance. It is about putting aside one's own needs for the good of another. It is not about prestige, power, fame or fortune, rather it is about the selfless love modeled by Jesus.

Mother Teresa modeled relational ministry on the streets of Calcutta; husbands' and wives' model relational ministry in marriage when they reflect back one another's goodness; employers' model relational ministry when they are willing to kneel down before each employee and wash their feet.

Jesus has called us to follow his example, to take into our hands human flesh, in all forms, even in its messiest, especially in its messiest, and cleanse it with our love and compassion.

We are to open our eyes and see each person before us as someone whose feet we can wash.

We are challenged to reach out and embrace the wounded person before us - the broken, bedraggled, sinful, lonely, imprisoned, and yes, even the most vulnerable - the mirror.

When we reach out to another through relational ministry, we are both touching and embracing the imperfections of another. That is where the healing of the heart and spirit transpires. It is through this love that we can transform the wounded and broken spirit in all of us and together come into the light of God's healing and forgiveness.

Washing each other's feet is about selfless, unconditional love in all forms. It is about our commitment to walk in the footsteps of Jesus, in response to his call... "Go now and Wash Each Other's Feet".

Opportunities for Personal Reflection and Discussion

1. What does washing each other's feet mean to you?

2. Why do you think Jesus washed the disciple's feet?

3. Has someone ever washed your feet either metaphorically or physically? What was the experience? How did it affect you?

4. Have you ever washed someone's feet with your compassion? What happened? How did they respond?

5. Do you know someone who washes the feet of other's regularly? What could you learn from them?

6. Whose feet could you wash today?

CHAPTER ONE
RELATIONAL MINISTRY

"There is only one place a person can be free from the perturbations of love. That place is one's coffin." C.S. Lewis

"What would make Christ go through what He went through for us? Love and all the rewards it brings- in warmth, companionship, fellowship and joy. Nothing brings more meaning to life than love. True love is what God is, and what we were made to know with him and with each other. So what will it be? The high cost of vulnerability of love, or the loneliness of isolation. A rock feels no pain, and an island never cries. But a son or a daughter knows a warm place in the family of God even if it hurts sometimes." John Fischer "A Rock Feels No Pain" in the Purpose Driven Life Daily Devotional

"We are called to love one another, in the flesh, in imperfection, broken-ness and sin. This is the love of relational ministry."

What is Relational Ministry?
The Language of Relationship

(Fr. Gale shares)

I had not heard the word "relationship" used in the sense of a close connection with another human being until 1973, when I was forty-five years old. All the years prior, even those when I was in the seminary, were about the individual relationship (the relationship with oneself) and one's relationship with God. I was taught about law and order and the superior power of the priest. It was all about me trying to fix people so they experienced more in life. The priest mentality of the time was always of the superior person ministering to the inferior person.

In addition, men weren't supposed to have feelings. Women had feelings, of course, but they were understood to be the weaker sex, so I learned to lie about the feelings I was experiencing. Inevitably over time they would surface in various ways. If you don't deal with your feelings, they will deal with you.

If you don't deal with your feelings, they will deal with you.

It was in 1973 on a Marriage Encounter weekend that I had my first real experience of God, and it was through Relational Ministry. The relationships I discovered between myself and the married couples and brother priests on this weekend changed my life. At one point dur-

3

ing the weekend, I was called upon to share my heart, my feelings, my pain. It was a huge challenge for me, but for some reason I opened up. I now know that reason to be the Holy Spirit, but at the time I couldn't understand why these feelings were bubbling up, actually coming out of my mouth, and I couldn't stop them. I trusted, I opened up, and I was both listened to and loved. My brothers and sisters accepted me for exactly who I was in that moment. No one tried to fix me or tell me how I should or should not feel. They just allowed me to be.

This was my conversion experience. It was twenty years after my ordination as a priest before I had my first experience of God! Not in Rome with the pope, not on or even near the altar of a church, but with my church family, the body of Christ, my brothers and sisters, on a marriage encounter weekend.

It was on this weekend that I first journaled about the first three steps of the Twelve-Step program of Alcoholics Anonymous, Al-Anon, and many such groups. I realized I was powerless. I turned my life over to the care of God as a loving father, and for the first time I understood him as a loving father.

That weekend was the first time I really heard and understood the word "relationship." I realized it was the first time I tuned into the whole notion of God speaking to me. He had never spoken to me before, and I was kind of resentful of that. But when I started listening to God, I discovered that he was always speaking to me; I was just on the wrong channel. He was speaking the language of relationship, a foreign language to me. When the student is ready, the teacher will appear!

God speaks to us constantly in the language of relationship. Father, Son, and Holy Spirit; three persons, one God, one love relationship—words we shied away from in the seminary and my early priesthood. We didn't get it. Today I have a different understanding. In fact, I have a whole different God—a loving father who calls me to him through relationship.

Relational Ministry is about accepting a person where they are, not where we think they should be. It is a process by which we act in love regardless of our personal desired outcome.

Relational Ministry is about accepting a person where they are, not where we think they should be.

(Tammy Shares)

Through my many years working in youth ministry, I am constantly blessed with the opportunity to meet extraordinary people. People like Mary. I first met Mary when we were teamed on a service project through youth ministry. Though I was the youth minister and Mary the student, I knew Mary would teach me far more than I could ever teach her. Those who know the hearts of teens know this lesson well. I was in the presence of holiness. Mary's heart was as pure as they come and her playful spirit had me laughing throughout the day. Our souls connected and we became close. Time passed and Mary went away to school. She was busy with the life of a collegiate and we kept in touch periodically.

One afternoon Mary surprised me with a phone call. I could hear the desperation in her voice as she choked on her trembling words. Mary confided that she had just found out one of her sorority sisters named Faith was scheduled to have an abortion the following morning. Mary cared deeply for Faith and upon hearing the news asked Faith if she would be willing to talk to someone before going through with the abortion. To Mary's surprise, Faith had agreed. Mary then asked if I would be willing to meet them near their college town. I of course agreed and made arrangements to get there as soon as I could.

We met at a restaurant and, after brief small talk, got into the reason for our meeting. Mary and I offered our desire to support Faith. We shared our concerns and our fears, as well as our desire to help her. We would walk through this unplanned pregnancy with her, by her side. We wanted her to know, she did not have to go through this alone.

Faith was distant at first, riddled with fear, anxiety, defensiveness, and anger. The child inside her was not part of her plan and she felt paralyzed in how to proceed in a new direction. To complicate matters, as often is the case in an unplanned pregnancy, Faith's parents did not know she even had a boyfriend, let alone was sexually active. In addition to that, her boyfriend was clear that he wanted nothing to do with being a father. He demanded she get an abortion or he would deny having anything to do with her. Faith was confident that her only option was to go through with the abortion. She challenged Mary and I saying there was no way we could possibly understand what she was going through. Faith was right. Neither Mary nor I had ever been in that exact situation. All we could do was listen, offer our support, and share ways we hoped Faith would let us walk with her, if she would let us.

We knew what Faith needed right now was an extended support system. We asked if she would allow us to drive with her to her parent's house, and we would be right beside her. Faith considered it, but then declined. "Not yet" she said, "but yes in time."

We could see the great turmoil Faith was struggling in. She was tense, her eyes tired, her face pale; I hurt for her. My soul truly ached wishing I could somehow comfort her.

Finally the conversation came to a close. Everything had been said. As we stood up to leave, Faith paused and said "I had not known what to expect this evening, but I am very thankful for both of you and for the sincere love I felt from you." I turned toward Faith and said "Faith, we are sisters in Christ, and I love you. There is nothing you could do that would make me stop loving you. Even though I just met you- we are all connected, Mary and I will help you in anyway you will allow us."

She put her arms around me and we hugged a genuine hug like many such embraces. But this hug transcended into a sacred moment of touch. I held Faith and as she moved in closer, I could feel her tears begin to pool on my shirt. As I held her I could feel the tension in her body release and at times I felt like I was all that was holding her up. She did not let go. I kept repeating as I held her, "It's okay, Faith. God loves you."

As I shut my eyes, I pictured Jesus cradling Faith in his arms, loving her through her pain, her turmoil, her confusion. I was honored in that moment that he would allow me to hold his daughter. When we parted, I left her with my phone number and asked her to use it anytime, day or night.

Now, I would love to tell you that everything worked out just as Mary and I had hoped. That Faith accepted our invitation to walk *with her through her pregnancy that she told her parents and they were supportive and that she had her baby and they lived happily ever after. That's not what happened.*

Mary called me the next day, impassioned in frustration and hurt. Through her tears she explained, "Tammy, Faith had the abortion. I am so hurt, so confused. She told me last night that she didn't want to go through with it. Why? Why? I don't understand!" I wish I had answers worthy of Mary's heartfelt questions. All I could do in that moment was to assure Mary that she had done everything she could do and that Faith was blessed to have a friend who loves her so much, unconditionally. I reminded Mary of how much Faith will continue to need her in the days, months, and years ahead. For we know all too well, there will continue to be many tough struggles on her journey. Mary's mom later told me that she had opened an email from her daughter that day that read, "Mom, there is another angel in heaven today."

Being in relationship with people is not without hurt, challenge and trial. They do not always have a story book ending. Relationships, like us, are messy. They are not always convenient, understandable, or logical. What relationships can be is this; empathic, caring, giving, accepting and loving. There are also times that Relational Ministry requires physical presence, such as the day with Faith. We could not have had the same experience with Faith over the phone, internet or voice mail. Relational Ministry places high importance on touch, eye contact, body language- physical presence. We wanted Faith to know she was loved, unconditionally, in spite of how we felt, or what we wanted for her.

That day with Mary and Faith reminded me of how God loves us – unconditionally, without question, without hesitation, without condition. There is nothing that we can do to mess that up. He also sends us people who can hold us up when we need to feel his arms.

Effective Relational Ministry is not a one-directional activity; it is a "we" relationship, a two-person relationship that is bi-directional and horizontal. It is both giving and receiving. Giving takes time, love, and willingness to extend oneself and receiving takes humility, vulnerability, acceptance, and openness.

Relational Ministry is not an outcome but a process. There will be many times in life when we don't get to choose or understand the influence we have as a result of an interchange, a conversation, a smile, a hug, or a listening ear. God uses all of our experiences, even the unexpected or painful ones as opportunities for Relational Ministry. We too can choose how we will accept people, places, and things that we cannot control. When we let go and give it to God, we are able to experience peace in all situations.

Opportunities for Personal Reflection and Discussion

1. What are some of your Relational Ministry stories?

2. Has someone ever accepted you for who you are not who they want you to be? Have you accepted someone that same way?

3. Is there a significant relationship you have learned from in your journey that has taught you how to treat others? What did they do that influenced you?

4. Is there a time you were able to listen to someone even if you did not agree with what they were saying? Have you ever felt listened to in spite of differences? What do you think the benefit is in this kind of exchange?

5. If there is someone who has impacted your life in a positive way? Could you write a note or make a call and tell them? This is a great way to affirm someone who has made a positive impact and let them know how they have influenced your life.

6. Identify a specific area in which you would like to grow relationally.

CHAPTER TWO
THE TOOLS OF RELATIONAL MINISTRY

"Acceptance is the answer to all my problems today. When I am disturbed, it is because I find some person, place, thing, or situation—some fact of my life—unacceptable to me, and I can find no serenity until I accept that person, place, thing or situation as being exactly the way it is supposed to be at this moment."
-The Big Book of A.A.

"You cannot live a perfect day without doing something for someone who will never be able to repay you."
-Sam Rutigliano, NFL Coach

"Let us love not in word or speech but in deed and truth."
—1 John 3: 18

There are many tools that help us in relational ministry. They include: acceptance, attitude, compassion, encouragement, empathy, humility, kindness, listening, problem solving, respect, understanding, and selfless love. Here are some of the tools in action.

The Tool of Acceptance

"Accepting and affirming that which is unacceptable within oneself, without self-blame or guilt, is to allow the unacceptable to be. This acceptance robs the unacceptable of power, and a new being emerges."

(Fr. Gale Shares)

When I was at a low time in my life, God sent me an angel named Sarah. I was not feeling very lovable and she turned that around. Sarah reflected back to me that there was a loving and lovable person dwelling within me. Sarah taught me the following through her love for me: "Accepting and affirming that which is unacceptable within oneself, without self-blame or guilt, is to allow the unacceptable to be. This acceptance robs the unacceptable of power, and a new being emerges." Sometimes it takes another to reflect back to us the love that was hidden. Someone like Sarah.

If we can embrace the gift of acceptance in regard to one another, we allow God to be in charge. When we realize we cannot change the action, behavior or thinking of another, we give them room to have their own spiritual experience, not the one we have mapped out for them. When we walk next to someone rather than in front of them telling them which way to go or behind them pushing them, we honor their relationship with God and his plan for them. We can in no way ever understand what another person is fully going through. When we let God be the pilot, we allow him to navigate while putting our faith and trust in him. We may find we even grow to appreciate each person's unique journey.

Acceptance as a pathway to Forgiveness and Healing

(Fr. Gale Shares)

Many have referred to me as the motorcycle priest due to my love of trips cross-country on my motorcycle. On one such trip, I was driving from Dallas to Connecticut with only a checkbook and a credit card at a time when credit cards were not as readily accepted as they are today and out-of-state checks were frowned upon. I quickly realized I was in need of food and had no means of attaining it. I then remembered a church I had once visited and decided to see a brother priest. I hoped to write him a ten-dollar check in exchange for cash to buy my needed food. Memory served me well this time, and I easily found the church.

Tired, thirsty, sweaty, hungry and exhausted, I approached the church door and knocked. Relieved to hear footsteps coming toward the door, I eagerly anticipated both the fellowship of a brother priest and an opportunity to obtain some much-needed cash. But what I was not ready for was the reception I would receive. Instead of a warm welcome, I was greeted by the priest screaming at me to go away. My attempt to identify myself and describe my situation was met with an increased resistance and growing anger which ultimately resulted in the door being slammed in my face.

Furious, I sped off down the road, raging at the inhospitable priest in my head. "Somehow, that priest will pay for this", I thought and I imagined the dozen or more letters I would write to the bishop. Like a bad song whose lyrics stick in your head, self-righteous anger accompanied me the length of my trip home.

Acceptance did not come easily, but then I had what I call a 'Holy Spirit moment'.

Once I was able to stop for a minute and reflect upon what my fellow priest might have been experiencing, my perspective changed. I thought about what might have happened the last time that priest had opened the door to a bedraggled stranger? Maybe he was threatened, robbed, or beaten. I then recalled that I did know a priest who had been killed reaching out to a stranger in need. Perhaps these thoughts were going through my colleague's mind when he had opened that rectory door.

At that moment, I experienced a surge of acceptance, peace, and understanding. Perhaps in the same situation, with the same experiences, I too might have responded the same way. Thanks to that 'Holy Spirit moment', I was able to not only grant forgiveness to my brother priest, but also to find compassion for him. It was then I was able to let the resentment and hostility go and begin true healing.

When we make the effort to understand that we could not possibly know where another person is coming from, we are able to extend our compassion and acceptance in any circumstance.

"Acceptance is the answer to all my problems today. When I am disturbed, it is because I find some person, place, thing, or situation—some fact of my life—unacceptable to me, and I can find no serenity until I accept that person, place, thing or situation as being exactly the way it is supposed to be at this moment. Nothing, absolutely nothing, happens in God's world by mistake. Unless I accept life completely on life's terms, I cannot be happy. I need to concentrate not so much on what needs to be changed in the world as on what needs to be changed in me and in my attitudes." - Big Book by Alcoholics Anonymous written by Dr. Bob and Bill Wilson

---

Acceptance is not to be confused with allowing ourselves to be abused or complacent. Rather accepting means the recognition that things are the way they are. It is admitting that we are powerless over the control of the universe, and we are willing to live within what is given to us. We can learn to lovingly respond to others by not re-acting to a negative situation. We also don't have to be around someone who is acting abusively. We can't control how another chooses to behave, but we can control how we respond. There are many situations we are incapable of fixing, or even changing. To accept the things we cannot change, to change only that which we can—allows us to love the person in spite of what they are going through and to love ourselves enough to not respond negatively hurting ourselves or someone else.

The Serenity Prayer

"Lord, grant me the serenity to accept the things I cannot change, the courage to change the things that I can, and the wisdom to know the difference."

The Tool of Empathy

A support group is a place people can come together to relate, share, grow and empathize with one another. More often than not, support groups are made up of people who are experiencing similar things in their lives— Eating Disorder Groups, Gambling Recovery, Alcoholics Anonymous, Divorce Recovery, Grief Support etc. There is a powerful connection with people experiencing similar things. They can empathize in a way sometimes others can't.

Empathy through a Support System

Our son Jac has a seizure disorder. One day, I was in complete despair and felt so alone. I called our wonderful neurologist and told

16

him my need for a support system. He thought it was a great idea! "Yes, we should have that Tammy! Why don't you go start one?" The fruit of need paid off. Jac's nurse Betsey said she would help. We entered the doors of the first support group meeting and found a packed room. Apparently I was not the only one with that need. I was overwhelmed with emotion to see so many others also searching for the same connection. We need each other, and we should never be ashamed to admit that.

We introduced ourselves and then opened it up for sharing from the group. A few people began to share about their children and their experiences. Then there was quiet in the room and a Spanish-speaking gentleman stood up. As we had not anticipated the need for a translator, he shared his heart partly in English and partly in Spanish, but everyone in the room was listening intently. He said he never knew there were others out there who felt as he did, and he could not contain his emotions any longer. He began to cry and through tears expressed his thanks. Gracious, muchas gracias, for being here, for sharing, and for showing me I'm not alone.

I realized in that moment that God had not inspired me to start a group for my own needs but for a greater need, a need that went well beyond what I could have envisioned, a need that connected us, a need that crossed over cultural or language barriers and that just allowed everyone to embrace the sameness of the journey we are on together.

Each of us has our own story to tell, our own experience, our own cause that could benefit from a support system that might identify our own unique needs. The universal truth is that we need each other. We were not meant to do this alone—God gave us each other.

"The sheep hear his voice; He calls them by name and leads them out." (Jn 10:3)

We are Jesus' sheep, his disciples, his beloved sons and daughters and he calls us by name. We are not on this journey alone.

The Tool of Attitude

> "Life is not the way it's supposed to be. It's the way it is. The way you cope with it is what makes the difference." Virginia Satir

A major tool affecting how we live out relational ministry is attitude. Attitude will affect our perception and our response. When we see the world as dark and gloomy, it will become so. When we seek God in the midst of all our circumstances and surroundings, he will be there. Attitude is a choice. Choose to have a good attitude and watch how the world around you changes. When we perceive our circumstances through the eyes of a victim, we become one. When we see our experiences as an opportunity to grow, they become a blessing. A positive attitude can have a monumental ripple effect in the way we can influence the lives of others.

Relational Ministry is Walking in Humility

WWJD-"What Would Jesus Do"- has become a familiar mantra. Charles Sheldon in his bestselling book, *In His Steps*, invites the question, "What would Jesus do in this situation if he were me?" Let's start by first looking at not only what Jesus would do, but what Jesus did? What did he model and call to us to follow...

The Humble Woman

> "A Pharisee invited him to dine with him, and he entered the Pharisee's house and reclined at the table. Now there was a sinful woman in the city who learned that he was at the table in the house of the Pharisee. Brining an alabaster flask of ointment, she stood behind him at his feet weeping and began to bathe his feet with her tears. Then she wiped them with her hair, kissed them and anointed them with the

ointment. When the Pharisee who had invited him saw this he said to himself, "If this man were a prophet, he would know who and what sort of woman this is who is touching him that she is a sinner. Jesus spoke, "Do you see this woman? When I entered your house, you did not give me water for my feet, but she has bathed them with her tears and wiped them with her hair. You did not give me a kiss, but she has not ceased kissing my feet since the time I entered. You did not anoint my head with oil, but she anointed my feet with ointment. So I tell you, her many sins have been forgiven; hence she has shown great love but the one to whom little is forgiven, loves little. He told the woman, your faith has saved you, Go in peace." (Lk 7: 36-39, 44b-47,50b).

In this gospel story, an uninvited prostitute comes into an elite banquet being thrown for Jesus by the societal upper class. The determined woman came and humbly knelt at the feet of Jesus. The self -righteous in attendance, blinded by their pride and ego, attempted to condemn her actions. Jesus quickly turned their judgment upside down and taught through her example.

She was the one person in the room who understood humility. Relational ministry is not about thinking oneself better than anyone else; it is not about judging others. Rather, it is about loving another with a pure, unselfish heart. The woman did not care what the others at the banquet thought of her. She cared only what Jesus thought. She subjected herself to their persecution because her greatest desire was to be with Jesus. She did not let fear overcome her faith.

When we love like this in our relationships, we become better able to recognize Jesus in our midst. Jesus as the homeless person with outstretched hands on the roadside, Jesus, as a senior citizen slowly driving on an aggressive freeway, Jesus as the clerk who is having a difficult day, Jesus as the waiter who got the order wrong, Jesus as the crack addict, the porn star, the ex-spouse, the abusive parent, or the person who has hurt you most. There was no place Jesus was unwilling to go, no person he would not touch, no one he was unwilling to forgive. Relational ministry challenges us to follow in these footsteps- The footsteps of Jesus.

Relational Ministry is a Self-less Love

"I use to look at people for how they could help me, but now my perspective is looking at how I can help them." Trent Dilfer, NFL QB

"A man fell victim to robbers as he went down from Jerusalem to Jericho. They stripped and beat him and went off leaving him half-dead. A priest happened to be going down that road, but when he saw him, he passed by on the opposite side. Likewise, a Levite came to the place, and when he saw him, he passed by on the opposite side. But a Samaritan traveler who came upon him was moved with compassion at the sight. He approached the victim, poured oil and wine over his wounds and bandaged them. Then he lifted him up on his own animal, took him to an inn and cared for him. The next day he took out two silver coins and gave them to the innkeeper with the instruction, "take care of him. If you spend more than what I have given you, I shall repay you on my way back." – Lk 10: 29-37

Many of us have heard the story of the Good Samaritan. We hear it in church. There is even a law named after it to protect a person who administers CPR to someone in need prior to the paramedics arriving. It is called the Good Samaritan Act. But how well are we actually living the Good Samaritan story in our own neighborhoods, churches, communities, and families?

How Samaritan like are we?

Carol was driving her kid's home from school one day when traffic began to back up. She looked ahead frustrated. Her girls whined to her

that she needed to hurry since they had gymnastics class and they did not want to be late again. Carol craned her eyes to see if there was an accident ahead. Carol then saw cars swerving around another car that had its hazard lights on. When Carol approached the car, she slowed and saw a father with his teenage daughter inside. She realized she could not just drive off without even asking if they might need help.

Carol slowed her vehicle and opened her window and the cars behind her began to honk angrily. She asked the man if he needed help, and his worried face looked relieved as he said, "Yes, Maam, I'm afraid we do." Carol offered to get the man some gas in a gas can and return. He thanked her and she was off. Carol returned shortly, the cars continued speeding by the man and his daughter in harried disgust. Carol warmly talked to the man as she could see how helpless he felt. He thanked her profusely and told her that he had been driving back and forth from the hospital to visit his dying mother and had been so tired he had mindlessly forgotten to fill up on gas... He tried to pay her. She said she would really like to help and that someday he will be able to help someone along the way too. She then asked the man how long he had been waiting for help before she stopped. To her surprise the man told her it had been well over 30 minutes. Carol could not understand how not even one other car would have stopped to help in that amount of time. She felt sad that her own community was too busy to take the time to help someone in need. Carol smiled at the man and his daughter as they waved and drove off.

When Carol got in her own car, her children were quiet. They looked at her and said "Mommy, we are glad you helped that man and his daughter today. That was the right thing to do, like Fr. Bruce tells us in church, to help those in need." Carol smiled and said, "That is exactly right girls." The girls continued,"But Mommy, there is one thing we can't figure out- why didn't anyone else stop to help too?" Carol knew it was a good question and asked the girls what they thought. "Well Mom, maybe they had gymnastics too and did not want to be late." Then they continued, "Mom I'm glad you let us be late. That was more important than gymnastics." Carol smiled in seeing the joy the girls were finding in helping someone. Only moments ago, they were absorbed into their own schedule, wants, and activities.

Now they were able to re-align their thinking and put someone else's needs before their own.

That night at dinner the girls told their Dad that the best part of the day was when Mommy let them be Samaritans.

Being a Samaritan is not always convenient, economical, practical, or without sacrifice. It is our call though and it does have its own rewards. Being a Samaritan is what Washing Each Other's Feet is all about.

How Samaritan like are our Communities?

Often our communities, even our churches, can become complacent in our attempt to do outreach. Recently a pastor of a church shared that at his own church outreach meeting the focus became fixated on how the needs of the outreach team were not being met. The mission of the group was to create service opportunities to reach the needs of the larger community.

The Pastor listened until he had all he could take. He sadly got up and left the room. He was perplexed wondering what was happening to the hearts of those in the room who had initially joined the group to reach out to others. This is a common reality of what can happen when an inward focus overcomes the desire for outward service. When the needs of others become secondary to our own needs, we are in danger of being like the priest and Levite who walked past the victim lying on the street.

Being a servant is not self centered, rather it is other centered. Today, our society is saturated with the concept of self help. We are not in disagreement that the necessity to care for oneself is important, but the pendulum often swings into the extreme where self focus dangerously overshadows selfless outreach.

It is almost counter culture to be other centered. Some even criticize it, confusing service with people pleasing. Sadly our culture often becomes so engrossed in our pursuit of success through prosperity and the desire for individual needs, that what becomes neglected is the compassion for others.

It is a misconception that we are able to achieve success in and of ourselves. The truth is that our best selves emerge when we are helping another. When we begin to define ourselves by illusions of self fulfillment through wants and desires, our spirit becomes increasingly empty and we long for it to be filled. It is not easy. Our society is plagued with temptations and misconceptions of immediate gratification, and being reinforced to never be satisfied with what we have been given. Relational Ministry is a different model than the one being exploited by mass media daily. This is the model of Jesus, the only model whereby one's spirit can truly learn to be satisfied.

Why is this message so important now? Current marriage statistics tell us that 51% of couples that marry today will end in divorce. Those would be discouraging odds if we did not have the hope of Jesus' example. Too often we hear the marriage mantra "What about me? What about my needs?" If we rewind the marriage vows, we see that it does not state "You should do this." Rather, it clearly states "I do". A healthy marriage is not based on finding the perfect spouse; it is about being a better spouse. Again, the responsibility lies within. Marriage is two people in one love relationship. The individual becomes a part of a team. Now it is a couple, and the focus switches from 'me' to 'we'.

Jesus epitomized the ultimate relational ministry example by asking us to "Love our neighbor as ourselves", and modeled humble service by washing the disciple's feet.

At the end of the Good Samaritan story, Jesus asked which of the men acted neighborly to the man left helpless. *He answered, "The one who treated him with mercy." Jesus then said to them, "Go now and do likewise." (Lk 10:29-37)*

Relational Ministry's foundation is the prayer of St. Francis. "Love more than you are loved."

St. Francis of Assisi: Peace Prayer

Lord, make me an instrument of your peace;
Where there is hatred, let me sow love;
Where there is injury, pardon'
Where there is doubt, true faith;
Where there is despair, hope;
Where there is darkness, light;
Where there is sadness, joy.

Grant that I may not so much seek
To be consoled as to console;
To be understood as to understand,
To be loved as to love;
For it is in giving that we receive,
It is in pardoning that we are pardoned,
And it is in dying that we are born to eternal life.

Eph. 6: 10-17

Questions for Personal Reflection and Discussion

1. What tools of Relational Ministry do you practice in your life today? What tools do you need to sharpen?

2. Is there something or someone you need to accept in your life today?

3. How can you apply the prayer of St. Francis in your relationships?

4. Has someone ever been a Samaritan to you? Describe what happened. Have you been a Samaritan in someone else's life? What do you think keeps people from helping others more readily?

5. What will you work on regarding your relationships with the neighborhood, church, and community today?

CHAPTER THREE
RELATIONAL MINISTRY IS WALKING TOGETHER

"The Lord sent them two by two."
-Lk 10:1

"Strive hard to be the best at what you do, while taking the needs of others into consideration."
-Roger Staubach, Retired NFL QB

"Being honest both with others and with yourself is treating others as you would like them to treat you."
-Jack Nickolaus, Retired Pro-Golfer

> "When Jesus saw his mother and the disciple whom he loved, he said to his mother, "Woman, behold, your son." Then he said to the disciple, "Behold, your mother." And from that hour the disciple took her into his home." (Jn 19:26-27)

Mary, the mother of Jesus, knelt at the foot of the cross where her son was being tortured and executed. The emotional excruciating pain Mary must have felt seems unimaginable. It was in this moment that Jesus reached out to his mother and his beloved disciple John and called them to comfort one another. We all know pain, suffering and injustice. We also can be comforted knowing Jesus will send people to walk with us; we are not asked to journey alone. When we throw up our hands and cry out to God in despair, "God I can't do this by myself." God looks upon us with compassionate and answers, "My child, I never meant for you to." Relational Ministry is about walking together.

Living Other-Centered is at the Core of Relational Ministry

(Karen's Story)

The youth group always visited the nursing home on the first Sunday of the month, and so it was the first Sunday. All the youth and adult volunteers gathered to board the bus. Upon arriving at the home, the students went room to room and invited the residents in to the main hall for bingo. Karen was one of the youth leaders who had been asked to come to help. It was her first time visiting and she felt unsure of herself in an unfamiliar situation. She found herself trying to inconspicuously edge her way to the back of the room where she could blend into the background. No such luck. Karen backed right into a man in a wheelchair who was perched in the back of the room as well. Startled, she turned quickly to find a friendly face.

"Hi there!" he said. "I'm Wayne." Karen introduced herself and the two engaged in conversation. Wayne had a dry sense of humor and was full of stories. Karen found herself absorbed in the fascinating conversation. After they had visited awhile, Wayne asked Karen if she would be kind enough to wheel him outside to enjoy the sunshine and the gentle breeze. She agreed and the two were off.

Karen had not realized how much time had passed and was surprised to see the others coming outside to re-load the bus and leave. They saw Karen and gathered around her and her new friend Wayne. Karen told Wayne they were leaving and how nice it had been to visit with him. Wayne told Karen the same and then paused. He hesitantly asked if there was one more thing she might do before she left. "Anything!" Karen said. "You name it Wayne." Karen was surprised by what Wayne wanted. He asked her to take off his socks. Karen willingly obliged, sat down at the foot of Wayne's wheel chair and began to take off his socks. Wayne then told her that his feet were hurting and he wanted to feel the breeze on them. Now the group outside was all gathering around Karen and Wayne watching what was taking place. Karen tried to gently pull off Wayne's socks but found they were very tight and seemed to be catching on his skin somehow. Karen continued with caution as she tenderly tried not to hurt Wayne. A few times Wayne winced in pain. Karen stopped and apologized, but he pleaded with her to continue.

When Karen had finally gotten Wayne's sock off, nothing could prepare her for what she saw. Wayne had open sores all over his feet. The hard calloused skin had broken open and blistered sores were oozing a mixture of puss and blood. All who were standing around watching were speechless. Karen continued trying to take off Wayne's *other sock even more cautiously now that she understood the severity of his condition.*

Once she got his socks off, Wayne let out a sigh of relief. He looked at Karen with such thankful eyes and whispered to her, "Thank you, no one here will touch my feet; they tell me they are too disgusting." Karen carefully took the part of Wayne's feet where there were no open sores and held them in her warm hands. She looked Wayne in the eyes and said, "Never have I seen more beautiful feet." Wayne chuckled and told her she desperately needed to get her eyes checked. Karen got up and went to hug Wayne goodbye when he drew her in close and whispered, "Thank you angel. I have been praying you would come." With tears in her eyes Karen said goodbye to Wayne and promised to visit again soon.

On the way home some of the students asked if Karen had been grossed out by Wayne's feet. She carefully answered, "Some of us are wounded on the outside for everyone to see; some of us are wounded on the inside. My insides looked like Wayne's outside. I took away the cloth that was keeping him from experiencing the breeze of touch, and he took away my fear and insecurity allowing me to feel the breeze of the Holy Spirit's touch on my heart.

Relational Ministry is a reciprocal exchange.

When we see with self-centered eyes, our vision is limited. But when we extend ourselves to others, our vision is limitless as seen through the eyes of love. When we move beyond ourselves and are ready to reach out to others, our own insecurities fall into the background. When we are able to operate from a place of love, we no longer have to react from a place of fear. Then everyone's basic needs are within reach. Our homes, our schools, our workplaces, and our communities could be sanctuaries—holy, sacred, peaceful places —where love is the foundation. We believe that by adapting these tools to our lives and relationships, peace is possible.

We know this is not easy, without risk, pain or challenge. We do however, believe it is possible.

John Fischer wrote an article in the **Purpose Driven Life Daily Devotional** called *"A Rock Feels No Pain."* In the article he says, "Love costs! Think of what Christ paid when he embraced us. Think of the pain the Son of Man endured in loving a lost and wayward humanity. Love is never without pain. When you sign on to being in relationship, you are signing on to being hurt. Count on it."

It is worth the risk. The greatest gifts in this life are our relationships that bring us to more fully experience the love of God. It's worth the risk when the reward is love.

The Relational Ministry Beatitudes

- Blessed are the poor in spirit- walk with them
- Blessed are they who mourn- comfort them
- Blessed are the meek- listen to them
- Blessed are they who hunger and thirst for righteousness- help them
- Blessed are the merciful- honor them
- Blessed are the clean of heart- seek them
- Blessed are the peacemakers- follow them
- Blessed are they who are persecuted for the sake of righteousness- support them
- Blessed are you when they insult you and persecute you and utter every kind of evil against you falsely because of me. Rejoice and be glad, for your reward will be great in heaven. Thus they persecuted the prophets who were before you." (Mt 5: 3-12)

Building a Relational Ministry Team

"By this all men will know that you are my disciples, if you have love for one another." ~Jn 13; 35

Relational Ministry is caring enough about someone to share with them good counsel. This kind of love transcends religious or political positions and accepts each person where they are. Here relationships are based on equality. The common ground is that we are all Children of God trying to do the best we can with the circumstances we have been given. In relational ministry, no one is greater. We are all servants called to serve one another. Our paths or our experiences may be different, but the destination is the same. Relational Ministry breaks down barriers and reduces the hardness of hearts. Dogmatism is obsolete and love complete. In order to relate to one another with such compassion, we are called to walk together. Each path is a spiritual journey. We are called to nurture not only our own growth, but the spiritual growth of others as well.

It is important to remember that in seeking to walk a spiritual path, it is not wise to go it alone. Good counsel is essential. How do we know if we are getting good council or not?

Good Council?

"You will know them by their fruits." (Mt 7:16)

A group of friends were sharing together when one person said that they were having a relationship problem. After disclosing some of the difficulty, a person from the group piped up and said, "I know what you need to do. You need to forget about them and you need to go and do something for yourself." It was not an uncommon remark in today's 'me-centered' culture. Fortunately, one of the other group members spoke up redirecting the feedback.

They shared that what they try to do in similar situations is to go and do something for someone else. They found by getting out of themselves, they were able to realize how insignificant their problem seemed in comparison, especially as they were volunteering at the cancer ward of the children's hospital. It is when we get out of self, not go further in that we are able to minister relationally.

How do you know when you are getting good counsel? If the counsel tells you to go and wash someone's feet, it is good council. Good counsel will provide you with a spiritual solution- a person who you see as a mentor.

What does a Mentor do?

There is a scene in the very beginning of the movie *Bugs Life;* the ants are busy at work storing food for the winter. The ants are joyfully working together and dutiful following the person right in front of them, when all of the sudden an unexpected leaf cascades to the ground creating a break in the line. Now this gap creates panic among the ants. They no longer know where to go or what to do and chaos ensues. Just as the ants begin freaking out, an ant who had been standing nearby on a hill watching what was going on came down from the hill and called to the ants, "Do not panic. Stay calm. Watch my eyes. Follow me. This is nothing compared to the twig of '93", he assured them, and soon the relieved ants were back on course.

That is a great visual describing what a mentor can provide: insight, perspective, wisdom, understanding, encouragement, compassion and direction that challenges us to grow and realign our path.

Remember what seemed so overwhelming, chaotic, and fearful to the ants on the ground was calmly remedied by the mentor ant that had the depth and clarity to resolve the situation. Sometimes we are too close and need someone with a broader perspective to guide us back on course.

The mentor–mentored relationship is an important partnership. Choose someone you are willing to listen to and learn from. Someone who has what you want regarding their spiritual walk.

Don't expect the mentor to be perfect. No one is. You are choosing them not to try to change them, but to seek change within yourself. Take responsibility for your own spiritual walk.

The first thing to do is to seek out a person you would like to be your mentor and ask them if they would be willing to work with you. Don't give up if they can't mentor you. This usually means they are who you thought and they are trying to honor their already existing commitments. Pray, and keep seeking.

Once the relationship has been established, then remain patient, humble and teachable. Spiritual growth does not happen overnight.

The mentor is not always your cheerleader telling you how great you are or that you are justified in your behavior. A good mentor will challenge you; will give you feedback on what you can do, not what another person needs to do. A healthy mentor does not allow you to act inappropriately or unkindly. They will compassionately guide you back to healthy relational ministry tools. Having a mentor is one of the greatest spiritual gifts you can have in your life.

(Tammy Shares)

One of my mentors is Pricilla. She is a saintly woman who amazes me. I will forever be striving to be more like her. One day I saw her at church and she greeted me with the warm smile she always does. "Hi Tammy, I hear my daughter is going to baby-sit for you tonight." My face fell and I said, "Actually, I am going to call her and cancel. I am not going out after all."

Pricilla inquired further. "I thought this was your husband's office party? What happened?" I explained that yes, it was his party, but

35

that we were in a fight. He really hurt my feelings and I could not get past it and pretend I was not mad at him. I already told him he is going without me. Pricilla listened intently. She let me get it all out and once I had finished, I quieted enough to let her respond. She then said, "So what time do you want Susan to be there again?" I thought she must not have been listening. I just told her I'm not going! Pricilla nodded as if reading my mind. "You know the right thing to do, Tammy. You will get dressed up, stand by your husband and be a godly wife tonight. Tomorrow you can be as mad as you want; I won't take that from you, but tonight you need to die to self." Ouch! That was so not what I wanted to hear. I wanted her to side with me, to tell me I didn't have to go, but that is not what my mentor did. My mentor looked me in the eyes and told me to 'die to self'. It doesn't get more clear than that.

"Relational Ministry is about dieing to self"

So what did the stubborn Irish girl do? I humbled myself and I listened to her wisdom. I washed his car, I got dressed up and we went to the party. On the way there he looked at me and smiled. "I really didn't think you would come." he said. "I know, I didn't think I would either." I responded. He then began to open up, "I'm really glad you did. You look beautiful." My anger softened and he continued. "I'm so sorry for the way I've acted, and the things I've said, I know it's no excuse, but I have been so stressed at work and I have unfairly taken it out on you. I hope you will find it in your heart to forgive me, I love you so much." That was all it took. There was no more anger or hard feelings. I apologized too and we proceeded to have one of the nicest nights ever. We danced and laughed and visited with lots of people. What would I have done without my mentor? I am stubborn. I probably would not have gone; I would have stayed mad, pouted, made things 10 times worse at home and missed out on a great time with my husband. A mentor can help in so many ways. Once you find one, you won't want to do it your way anymore.

Team Building

Having one mentor is great. Having a team is even better! The quote "It Takes a Village" comes to mind. Wise council comes in many forms and through many voices. The more we open ourselves up to listening to the wisdom of others, the more teachable we become. Chances are you already have a team in place, just grow the concept. Here is an example. Todd has a doctor, a personal trainer, a therapist, a chiropractor, a best friend, a tennis partner, a financial advisor, a sponsor in a 12 step program, and a brother he adores. Todd has a team of people who care about him in place. He has several people he can seek trusted counsel from and he can build from there.

How to get started building your team?

Think of yourself as a quarterback assembling your defensive line. You will want to pick strong leadership. If they are not in fit condition, you will suffer. Same goes for your mentor leadership team. Choose healthy people to surround you. Not perfection, but those devoted to walking an authentic spiritual path. It is not uncommon for the relationship to transition into friendship. If this happens, continue to add to your team people who will guide you honestly. Sometimes the equality of friendship can interfere with the impartiality of the mentor relationship. Remember someone helping you on a spiritual journey does not always tell you what you want to hear. Think of the mentor as the ant on the hill. He is not always the ant next to you just as lost. Be purposeful about these relationships and make the time. Your spiritual life is worth it.

How to combat stagnation?

There are many challenges that allow us to become stagnant in our spiritual journey. Consider working out for example. When a person works out regularly, they begin to get stronger, not immediately but gradually over time. If you are strength training, you might start with a lighter weight and over time build upon that. In the beginning the lighter weight feels enormously heavy. After time, it becomes almost too easy and you have to add more weight to get the same effect. You are stronger now. Your body has adapted and is ready for more. If you don't add more resistance, your body becomes stagnant. You have to increase the pressure to make it grow stronger yet again. You can choose how you want to change it up- add different exercises, more repetitions, or heavier weight. The important thing is that you are changing up what your body has become accustomed to. It is the same with our spiritual walk.

In order to constantly grow, we will be challenged to initiate change. It is not always easy. Like exercise, there are times we will get uncomfortable and not want to do the work. Like exercise, there are times we will not see the results fast enough and want to give up questioning why are we putting ourselves through this at all? Isn't it a waste of time? But like exercise, when we persevere and become willing to get a little uncomfortable, we ultimately get stronger, healthier and better able to handle additional pressure, whether it is in strength training or in our personal lives. Start assembling your team today and get ready to grow!

Everyone Can't Be in Your Front Row

Life is a theater - invite your audience carefully. Not everyone is holy enough and healthy enough to have a front row seat in our lives. There are some people in your life that need to be loved from a distance. It's amazing what you can accomplish when you let go, or at least minimize your time with draining, negative, incompatible, not-going-anywhere relationships/ friendships/fellowships

Observe the relationships around you. Pay attention to which ones lift and which ones lean? Which ones encourage and which ones discourage? Which ones are on a path of growth uphill and which ones are going downhill?

When you leave certain people, do you feel better or feel worse? Which ones always have drama or don't really understand, know and appreciate you and the gift that lies within you?

The more you seek God and the things of God -- the more you seek quality, the more you seek not just the hand of God but the face of God -- the more you seek things honorable -- the more you seek growth, peace of mind, love and truth around you, the easier it will become for you to decide who gets to sit in the Front Row and who should be moved to the balcony of your life.

You cannot change the people around you... but you can change the people you are around! Ask God for wisdom and discernment and choose wisely the people who sit in the front row of your life.

Questions for Personal Reflection and Discussion

1. Do you have someone in your life that has mentored you?
2. Have you ever felt the presence of Jesus in the midst of pain through another person?
3. Do you currently have a mentor?
4. Who would be on your team? List them. What characteristics do they have that will help you in your journey?
5. What do you need to do to put your team together today?
6. Who is someone who you can help as a mentor today? What can you offer to do to help them?

Chapter Four
Barriers to Relational Ministry...

"Why do you see the speck in your brother's eye, but do not notice the log that is in your own?"
-Mt 7:3

"Judge not, that you may not be judged."
-Mt 7:1

"Success is to be measured not so much by the position that one has reached in life as by the obstacles that one has overcome while trying to succeed."
-Booker T. Washington

B arriers to Relational Ministry include: judgementalness, ego, control, fear, criticism, projection, shame and blame. Let's see how these influence relational ministry.

Relational Ministry is not Judgmental

Becky and Jon were thrilled when their firstborn son, Christian, turned four; the age children could join the community soccer team. Although Christian seemed more eager to pick flowers than participate in the various drills during practice, his parents always had their camera ready just in case. As it turned out, they saved a lot of money on film that season.

One child, Nick, stood out from the others. Not because of his size or talent, but because of his unusual hair—dark on the sides with a pronounced swath of bleached blond across the top, just like the more statement-oriented teenagers. Becky would hear many of the parents whisper, "Why would they do something like that to his hair? I can see parents of teens fighting that battle, but parents of a four-year-old . . . really!"

Even though Becky didn't say anything, she couldn't help but secretly wonder the same thing. She mentally crossed Nick's parents off the list of those they might become close friends with. They obviously had different parenting perspectives. Becky thought that she was being a good Christian by not joining in the criticism. But really she too was judging even in her silent thoughts.

One Saturday morning, Becky and Jon's neighborhood was hosting a community garage sale. Becky looked up from her recyclables and recognized a familiar two-toned head of hair. It was Nick, playing with her son Christian. Soon Nick's parents walked up and greeted Becky and Jon. As the conversation progressed, Becky couldn't restrain her curiosity any longer and asked about Nick's hair. Becky was not prepared for what Nick's mom, Kari, told her... Kari openly responded, pulling up a chair: "I will be happy to tell you, but I can't promise I won't cry."

Kari then went on to explain how her younger brother, Kent, a senior in high school, was in a very serious car accident from which he was not expected to live. He was in intensive care at the hospital, and Nick was too young to go visit him. Nick idolized his Uncle Kent and wanted to be just like him in every way. Kari continued, "Nick approached me and said, "Mom, I know what I can do to let Uncle Kent know that I am thinking about him. I could do my hair like his, and you can take my picture to him. To remind him I am thinking of him even though they won't let me see him. You can tell him that every time someone asks me about my hair or when I see it in the mirror, I will remember to stop and pray for Uncle Kent. My hair color will be like a part of him being with me at all times."

Humbled and now in tears, Becky was reminded how easy it is to judge someone from the outside and just how wrong her own assumptions had been.

Striving to overcome the temptation to judge another is one of the key challenges of Relational Ministry. Becky learned this once she became willing to listen to another's story without judgment. Becky and Kari, and their boys, are extremely close friends today. This reiterates the point of what Becky would have missed out on had she stayed stuck in her judgementalness.

Stone Throwing

"Then the scribes and the Pharisees brought a woman who had been caught in adultery and made her stand in the middle. They said to him, "Teacher, this woman was caught in the very act of committing adultery. Now in the law, Moses commanded us to stone such women. So what do you say?" They said this to test him, so that they could have some charge to bring against him. Jesus bent down and began to write on the ground with his finger. But when they continued asking him, he straightened up and said to them, "Let the one among you who is without sin be the first to throw a stone at her." Again he bent down and wrote on the ground. And in response, they went away, one by one, beginning with the Elders. So he was left alone with the woman before him. Then Jesus said to her, "Woman, where are they? Has no one condemned you?" She replied, "No one, sir." Then Jesus said, "Neither do I condemn you. Go, and from now on do not sin anymore." -Jn 8:2-11

In this story Jesus defies the law, which stipulates that the woman be stoned to death. Instead, he extends himself for the woman, embracing her with his love, pointing out a path on which she might continue her spiritual journey in the light of love, hope and forgiveness.

He does not condemn. He overrules the judgment of those who dragged the woman to him. But Jesus accepts her, comforts her, and leads her on a path to spiritual recovery. This is the path of Relational Ministry, a path that follows Jesus by removing all judgment from our relationships.

Keeping Your Side of the Street Clean

"Stop judging, that you may not be judged. For as you judge, so will you be judged, and the measure with which you measure will be measured out to you. Why do you notice the splinter in your brother's eye, but do not perceive the wooden beam in our own eyes? How can you say to your brother, 'Let me remove that splinter from your eye,' while the wooden beam is in your eye?" -Mt 7: 1-4

(Fr. Gale shares)

I was about to board a plane in Chicago when I noticed someone whose physical appearance tweaked the judgmental streak in me. I was not in the best of moods to begin with because I was in Chicago to see some friends and my plans were interrupted by a call that necessitated my immediate return to Dallas.

As I stood waiting for the announcement to board the flight, I noticed that there was a gentleman standing next to me. It immediately occurred to me that I didn't like his over-large blue suit, or the oddly patterned tie he was wearing, or the way he was standing, or even his bald head. On top of that, I was very turned off by all the rings on his fingers.

Why I even noticed all this I don't know. Not being a very observant person, I rarely notice such details, but this time I did. And I proceeded to pass all kinds of judgments on the poor fellow as a result, no doubt feeling very self-righteous. I would never wear such gaudy rings on my fingers!

A little while later, we boarded the airplane, and guess who ends up sitting right next to me? Yes, the bald, fashion-challenged ring man. No sooner had we settled into our seats when he turned to me and said, "Father, it is not by accident that I am sitting right next to you. I saw you at the airport and I asked God to let me sit next to you so I could talk to you." (This was before I learned not to wear clerical garb when traveling!) I immediately thought, Oh Lord, I'm stuck for this entire flight from Chicago to Dallas with this odd duck sitting next to me, and he thinks it's all God's will!

It got worse. He then proceeded to tell me that he is a professor of the occult at The University of North Texas. So now not only did I have to listen to this guy, but I would probably have to defend my religion as well. As I had feared, he immediately started talking about Jesus and Christianity.

Hoping to avoid a heated argument, I casually mentioned that I am not supposed to judge him for what he believes. His response was completely unexpected. "Father, that's not what the Bible says. It goes quite a bit deeper than not judging another. What the Bible says is that you should not judge, period. In fact, in Matthew, Chapter 7,

Jesus says quite forcefully, 'Do not judge.' It starts with you judging yourself. If you are judging yourself, Father, then you must be judging me."

His words were like the proverbial two-by-four between the eyes. Here I was judging myself because of all these feelings I was having. I felt angry about the emergency call to return to Dallas which had interrupted my plans with friend. I felt judgmental about this man before I even knew anything about him, and I had increasingly negative feelings now that I was learning something about him, therefore judging myself more for having all these feelings. Then coming face-to-face with this strange person telling me that I must not judge myself or others!

What a revelation all this was! Judge not others. Judge not self. For in judging others, you are really judging yourself.

We judge ourselves negatively every time we make judgments about the feelings that we have. What's the healthy response to all this? To honestly acknowledge how we feel, particularly with the people with whom we are in relationship. We don't have to tell the whole world what we're feeling (thankfully!), but we do need to be open about our feelings (after we have accepted them ourselves). When we do so, we will be truly ministering to each other as we learn to listen and to accept each other.

I will forever be grateful to God for giving me the wisdom of a professor of the occult in a goofy blue suit and as many rings as fingers to teach me about not judging self or others.

"There but for the grace of God go I."

Have you ever said "I'll never do that" and then you find yourself doing that exact thing? None of us are exempt from living life on life's terms. We have a choice to judge and condemn or to accept and love. We can throw the stones or we can put down the stones and choose to have compassion and understanding. Truth is that most times what we are judging outwardly in another, we are fearing inwardly about ourselves. Many times projecting is what people will choose, so that they don't have to acknowledge their own sinfulness or shortcomings.

It's doesn't work though. By acknowledging and pointing out another's defects, it only makes our own surface. "There but for the grace of God go I" is a reminder that each of is wounded, each of us is capable of descending to a place of fear, rejection, and judgementalness.

Our answer is to love one another as God loves us, with all our imperfections.

A lesson in love

While Tracie was in college, she took a course titled "Family Dynamics of Addiction." She learned much about family systems, helping her to be much more empathetic. One of the course assignments was to attend a dozen different Twelve-Step programs such as: Alcoholics Anonymous, Overeaters Anonymous, Al-Anon, Gamblers Anonymous, etc.

One beautiful Saturday afternoon after a previous night of partying with her sorority sisters, Tracie decided to fulfill one of the obligatory twelve-step meetings which was being held at a nearby park. She arrived early and decided to stay in her car and wait for the participants to arrive. The first to arrive was a young man; close in age to Tracie, scruffy in appearance with long stringy hair, and, a little intimidating to her. "I do not belong here" Tracie thought to herself as she sat in her late model sports car, dressed in her preppy clothes, the memories of a night with her sorority sisters still fresh in her mind, and a headache to ensure that the memory wouldn't fade too quickly. Tracie wondered whether she should attend that meeting, given the kind of people showing up. Maybe she could find another Twelve-Step program to observe; one she might be better able to relate to.

As time went on, more people arrived and Tracie decided to fulfill the course requirement and join them. Scared and uneasy, her chest pounding with anxiety, she did her best to sneak in unobtrusively along the outskirts of the assembling crowd. As she stood there with growing discomfort, a gentle hand touched her shoulder and a voice said, "Hi, I'm Bruce, I don't think I've seen you before. Are you new?" Tracie turned to meet this gentle stranger's eyes and, of course, it was the scraggly, long-haired young man she had been watching from the distance of her car.

He invited her to sit by him, and without hesitation she did. She was, in fact, quite appreciative of the warm welcome, the extended hand, and the kind invitation. Bruce then invited Tracie to participate and read a meditation. He certainly knew how to welcome others, she thought, and how to put them on the same level, instantly making them part of the group and allowing them to experience belonging.

This welcoming stranger, with his gentle eyes, warm touch, and willingness to reach out, affected Tracie in a truly prophetic way. As the meeting unfolded and various participants shared their feelings and what was really going on inside them, Tracie was touched beyond words. When it was Bruce's turn to share, he spoke of his appreciation for his disease of alcoholism and how he was so grateful to be sober for ten years.

Ten years! Tracie was surprised. She thought he had been out partying all night; he looked absolutely worn out. And then she remembered who had been the one out partying all night the previous evening, and she lowered her head. The person she was judging from afar, judging based on outward appearances, was the one who acted with compassion and love. He had been the one who withheld judgment on her, a hung-over sorority girl with an over-sized bow in her hair. He could have judged her, but he didn't.

What happened to Tracie that day was a powerful conversion experience. Bruce looked upon Tracie with the eyes of Jesus and she was humbled through the experience. Today Tracie is an active and grateful member of a Twelve-Step program- by the Grace of God, and in large part due to Bruce's warm welcome that spring day.

By striving to be nonjudgmental, we focus on the fact that we don't know what others are going through, what they go home to each night, what their experience was growing up, what attitudes and perceptions were instilled in them, what injustices they have suffered, what they endure on a daily basis. Being free of judgment allows more room in our heart for compassion, forgiveness, and love.

Jesus calls us not to judge, but rather to love. The more tolerant we are of our own imperfections and weaknesses, the more tolerant we are of others.

The Barrier of FEAR
(False Expectations Appearing Real)

We all have fears and they manifest themselves in different ways in all of our lives. The fear of being judged is one of the underlying reasons we avoid sharing our feelings with others. Negative thoughts such as: "I am afraid I will be rejected," "I shouldn't feel that way," "I will be manipulated," "I'll be taken advantage of," "I'll be thought less of," "I'll be laughed at," "They'll figure out the real me and won't like me", keep us from experiencing the blessing of sharing our authentic self in relationship with another person and allowing them to do the same with us. It is a false notion that we are supposed to be self sufficient and that it is a sign of weakness to reveal our imperfections or need for another. This is upside down. The truth is the healthiest, most successful people know how to reach out for help and know that true intimacy involves working with others. Fear immobilizes us where as faith empowers us.

Four Relational Barriers of EGO
(Edging- Out- God)

1. Ego stands as one of the primary barriers to relationship. It is helpful to remember that Jesus, who never spoke publicly until he was 30 years old, was not motivated by ego in anyway. Jesus was the example of being other-centric rather than egocentric.

2. When we operate out of our egos, we are; in fact, living in fear—fear of not having enough, fear of losing what we

have, fear of not being accepted, fear of not being loved. When we act out of that fear, we get into blame, shame, criticizing, grasping, and punishment. Politicians often talk to our fears and then present themselves as the persons who can protect us from the very fears they just projected onto us. Trust is a bridge that helps us over the barrier of ego and its underlying fear. Trust in Jesus, trust in self, trust in one another.

3. If we only tell each other what we think the other person wants to hear, or what we think we should say as opposed to what we really feel, we are not being true to our own self, therefore not being authentic. But this takes risk—it takes both truth and trust within our relationships. It takes opening up and letting go of preconceived ideas and 'shoulds', and fears of the ego.

4. Have you ever been hurt by something someone has said about you? It feels like being kicked in the stomach, like having the wind knocked out of you. It makes you question yourself and the other person as well. A first reaction might be to become defensive. We can accept the challenge of accepting that remark as just someone's feedback—good or bad, deserved or undeserved, hurtful or helpful. It is simply feedback, one person's perspective. How we handle feedback can serve as a growth opportunity, allowing us to reach further into our potential. Remember, we don't have to take on everyone's feedback- take what you like and leave the rest.

Humility vs. Ego

(Tammy Shares)

My husband, Brett, and I have been extremely blessed to have the greatest neurologist in the world for our son Jac, Dr. Mauricio Delgado, head of Pediatric Neurology at the world-renowned Texas Scottish Rite Hospital for Children in Dallas. Jac suffers from irretractable seizures and has been under the care of Dr. Delgado since he was 2 years old. Dr. D. has always emphasized that we all work together as Jac's Team! He even factors in our input as parents into the treatment plan. This approach allows our family to be part of the process, and in a world in which parents most often feel powerless, there comes a moment of empowerment.

Families of special needs children spend a considerable amount of time in hospitals and with medical personnel. Since dealing with doctors is very common in our world, many personalities have crossed our path.

During one hospital stay, Jac had just gotten out of surgery and was not doing well. Physically he was at an all-time low, which of course left us emotionally spent. During a stressful seizure episode, an interchange took place with an on-call neurosurgeon. We felt caught in a trap of miscommunication, ego-centered dialogue, and reactive communication, which did not allow for listening, hearing, or responding to the needs of our child.

Many of us can relate to such unpleasant encounters, regardless of whether it was in a doctor's office or in a customer service line. You feel helpless, despondent, mistreated, and unheard. Thoughts race through your head: "What could I have said differently? Where did that conversation go wrong? Why did they think it was okay to talk to me that way?"

In the situation with Jac, we tried to be kind but also needed to advocate on behalf of our son. We were his voice and his needs were going unmet.

Then our super-hero-doctor once again came to our rescue! Dr. Delgado entered the situation as our white coated knight and as Jac's angel. He eloquently and firmly advocated on Jac's behalf and brought Jac the relief he needed. He more than rescued him; he saved him.

Later, he apologized to us on behalf of his colleague's disposition and shared his frustrations about how some in the medical communities abuse their authority and mistreat those they have vowed to help. He talked about how he has heard patients discuss certain doctors who do not have good bedside manner. Dr. Delgado suggests such doctors should take a class to help them since the nature of their job does in fact put them at people's bedside. He said there is no excuse for ego in a helping profession. Through Dr. Delgado's compassion, advocacy and caring heart, we were able to get Jac's needs met. We are continuously overwhelmed with gratitude for someone who cares with such love. We pray that you too will know a Dr. Delgado in your life and that all of us will strive to follow his example extending ourselves for the needs and advocacy of others.

One thing about Dr. D's humility is that he never pretends his wisdom or strength comes from him. He is quick to point to his power source - God. Dr. Delgado reminds our family to pray and humbly tells us that he himself can only do small things, but it is God who we need to seek to do miraculous things.

Humble people do not take credit; rather they acknowledge their gifts as being from God. Humble individuals always remain teachable, never assuming that they know everything. Jesus calls us to wash each other's feet using our own unique gifts and talents and that is precisely what Mauricio Delgado does for our son Jac and our family every day.

The following story contrasts the ego driven neurosurgeon with a humble servant reaching out with compassion in service to someone else.

Noah was no stranger to hospitals. Since the day he was born with a disability, he had been in and out of them, going through surgery after surgery and medicine after medicine.

During one of Noah's hospital stays, he became violently ill following a treatment that did not agree with him and the hospital room floor was the recipient of his sick stomach. Emily, a hospital employee in charge of keeping the rooms sanitary, came in the room to check on Noah just as he was getting sick. Emily immediately got to work coming to the aid of Noah. She worked by his bed and mopped the floor below. Noah's mom, Heidi, interceded quickly, trying to take responsibility for her son's mess. She told Emily that she herself would clean up. Emily smiled at Heidi's thoughtfulness and continued to clean. Heidi offered again to help and pleaded with Emily to just rest and that she would get to it later. Emily again thanked Heidi but assured her that she was there to help. Emily wasn't asking Heidi to bow down before her. She was asking Heidi to allow her to serve in the way she had been called, to wash Heidi and Noah's feet. Many of us can relate to Heidi's resistance. Like, Peter in the washing of the feet story.

"No Lord, I should wash your feet."

One of the most challenging lessons for many of us is to allow ourselves to be humble enough to have our feet washed. Emily was Jesus to Heidi that day, and ultimately Heidi surrendered to the temptation of Peter and allowed Emily to wash her feet by cleaning up Noah's mess.

Looking at these two stories, we find ourselves confronted with this question: Who is Washing Feet? Is it the actions of an arrogant neurosurgeon that didn't have the time or willingness to listen to parents who were concerned for their child? Or is it Dr. Delgado a Pediatric Neurologist who makes house calls and takes the time to listen, support and walk with each of his patients and their families. Is it The Ego demanding respect of one doctor who assumed he knew enough about a situation to assess it without regard to the parent's and the child's needs? Or is it the humility of Emily, a humble servant, mopping up someone else's vomit? Relational Ministry is about the humility of Emily's and Dr. Delgado's, who daily live out high touch ministry in our high tech world.

The Barrier of Control

Let's look at a couple who is well versed in the high tech tools of force and control and is attempting to apply them to their child. Sam is a pre-teen whose attitude and behavior have been brought to the attention of the school administrators and his parents. His parents respond in the way they think will yield results, not using relational ministry tools. The parents tell Sam he needs to shape up and threaten him with a litany of consequences he will have to endure if he does not comply. When Sam's attitude does not change the couple begins the process of taking things away—CD player, computer, television, video games, friends, activities, and so on — what does Sam do?

Typically, he rebels, covertly or overtly, and his negative behavior continues. We are able to see how the directive of force and control is not going to reap the desired outcome for either the parent or the child. Relational Ministry is not about control, manipulation, or force that exists in directions like: "How many times do I have to tell you?" "You never listen." "You will never change." "You are not going to wear that, you look like..." – etc. If controlling people could only see that their actions are not succeeding, nor is their desired outcome forthcoming. Anytime a person feels as if they are reduced to simply an object of direction, they will push away and there will be conflict.

Attempting to control another person may seem like an easy, expedient way to get immediate results; in actuality, it usually yields the opposite effect.

If the manipulative or micromanaging boss could learn some of the basic principles of respectful empowerment—giving his or her employees the resources they need to do the job, establishing clear guidelines for what needs to be done while allowing for alternative methods of accomplishing outcomes, demonstrating personal interest in employees' lives, and putting in place clear processes for communication—absenteeism and employee turnover would decrease, employee attitudes would improve, and production would increase. Unfortunately, too many bosses rule by intimidation, stalking the employees and threatening that the firings will continue until morale improves.

Today there are numerous workshops teaching those in the workplace how to relate to one another with respectful relational ministry tools. The tools help empower employees by equipping them with leadership skills that encourage team building, supporting, communicating and sharing feedback with one another. As part of a team, the goal is about the good of the whole not just individual. One challenge is when a person in charge is threatened and operates from reactive fear unwilling to share control. Many fear that by letting go, even a tiny amount of control, chaos will ensue. The best way to influence another is to demonstrate your unconditional positive regard for that person. Control pulls apart; Love builds alliances—in marriages, in families, and in the workplace. Once we have the tools of relational ministry, we can apply them in all areas of our life.

Opportunities for Personal Reflection and Discussion

1. Is there anyone you have mis-judged? What can you do to amend your thinking or the relationship?

2. Do you know someone who uses force, control or manipulation to get their way? Could they be helped by the tools of relational ministry?

3. Have you ever experienced the challenges of communicating with someone who is caught in the trap of pride and ego? How did you deal with it? Was it effective?

4. How can you keep yourself from falling into the trap of resorting to barriers of relational ministry?

5. Do you know someone like Dr. Delgado or Emily in your life? Have you told them lately how much you appreciate them? Take the time to write them a letter and tell them.

Chapter Five

Relational Ministry Is High Touch in a High Tech World

"We are participants in a vast communion of being, and if we open ourselves to its guidance, we can learn anew how to live in this great and gracious community of truth. We can, and we must if we want our sciences to be humane, our institutions to be sustaining, our healings to be deep, and our lives to be true."
-Parker Palmer; Let Your Life Speak

"Look at my hands and my feet, that it is I myself. Touch me and see, because a ghost does not have flesh and bones as you can see I have."
-Luke 24: 39

"There is no exercise better for the heart than reaching down and lifting people up."
-John Andrew Holmes

L et's think about the methods we are currently using in our relationships today. Are we trying to build world peace, end world hunger, and make everyone love one another by using the same tools that we use to advance technology?

When we are talking about love, we need to talk about the tools of relationship, not the tools of technology based on force and control. Connecting to the heart is what high touch relational ministry is about. It is seeing the humanness of the person before us, flesh and blood, whole and wounded, living in the here and now, needing to be listened to, heard, understood, accepted, and touched.

Where to begin? What is the most important relationship any of us have? Our relationship with God. The first question then would be- how much am I willing to invest of myself in this relationship: Time, Energy, Trust, Commitment, etc. How much am I willing to let go of the control and let God be in the driver seat? That is the most important place to start.

Next we look at our relationships with others and ask ourselves honestly: Am I willing to extend myself—physically, emotionally, spiritually, and every other way—for the good of the other? Am I willing to see that wounded person in front of me as one deserving of my total, undivided, empathetic attention? Am I willing to discard the tools of the old technology, which can be successful when applied to objects, and replace them with tools of relationship?

High Tech vs. High Touch

Advances in medical technology have changed the lives and even saved the lives of many who just a generation ago could not have been helped. Probably all of us know someone—a relative, a friend, a work associate—who has benefited from recent advancements in open heart surgery, cancer detection, neonatal care, or other areas that baffle us by their great strides of technological advancement.

The Vagus Nerve Stimulator is one example of the high tech medical advancements. This titanium disk, the size of a cracker, is imbedded behind the pectoral muscle in a patient's chest wall. It is then connected to a wire that wraps around the Vagus Nerve. The battery is activated by a computer system that initiates electrical impulses to the brain through a battery-operated magnetic host. This is the first breakthrough in treating seizures without anti-epileptic medication in over a hundred years. This recent invention has had a significant amount of success in helping to decrease both the amount and length of seizures in many, and its use has recently been extended to help those with depression and other neurological conditions.

High Touch—High Tech Balance:

It is also true that our society's emphasis on technology has a need to be balanced. Without such tools, our ability to connect relationally could be seriously compromised. For example, have you ever tried to make a simple phone call—a rather commonplace task not so long ago—and find yourself deeply embroiled within a frustratingly complex maze from which there appears to be no escape?

Your goal is to speak to a human being. Ask a very simple question and you are confronted with: the pre-recorded message that spews out confusing instructions related to the pushing of various buttons directing us to persons unknown, the access of which only leads to more buttons leading to more instructions, and more time lost. After this endless litany of directions, none of which appear to address the specific question you have in mind, you are left in such frustration that you hang up and decide to do something else.

No doubt we have all had similar frustrating experiences. In order to save time and/or money, our society is reduced to speaking to machines and recordings that at times replace a conversation between two people. We have conference calls that we don't need to be present for, internet correspondence; we have drive thru banks, cleaners, restaurants, and even popular coffee establishments. These again can be modern conveniences and they can also be ways we wind up void of human contact all together

There are times when it's appropriate to take advantage of high tech tools. For example, letting the telephone answering machine pick up messages during the family meal is a great idea.

There is a time and place for email, voicemail, computers, and the tools of high tech. We just need to try to maintain a healthy balance. Honor both your time and that of others by scheduling with consideration and planning. Continually realigning your personal goals allows you to regularly connect with the significant people in your life. We know this is not always easy, but most meaningful things aren't. The blessings of relational ministry are well worth the investment you put into it.

Dealing with people is not a science we can master, nor should we treat it as such. We cannot have the same relationship with a machine as we do with another person. Have you ever had a misunderstanding via email? Something that was misinterpreted or misunderstood? It happens! This is one of the many challenges we face when we try to use the tools of technology as our primary means of communication. There can be much lost in the translation.

Listening is a high touch skill

Let's look at the skill of listening. We are not able to listen to what a person is saying over an email or text message in the same way we are able to listen to them in person. In person, we can see their eyes, hear their voice inflection, watch their body language, and understand their gestures. We can sense some of what they are expressing through their non-verbal communication. Active listening is an extremely important part of relational ministry.

(Fr. Gale shares)

"Every year I facilitate a men's retreat and I always begin the same way - by talking to men about listening.

I tell them that we need to stop the movie reel that constantly plays in our head because we are not really listening when it's going on.

When people in our lives, especially women, begin to express their feeling to us males, we automatically go into fix it mode. Men are a rolodex of fixers; we have a solution on hand for each problem. All of us want to answer back, share our part and think of what to say next. We tune out, tune in, and turn off.

On the weekend, we practice listening to each other, and then we reflect back. A man who has been married for 15 years shared with me that he had never really listened to his wife. He went home after the first night of the retreat and really listened; he reported back that he had incredible results.

Listening is the most redemptive element in healing; it makes us feel special, heard, and paid attention to. We need to hear for us, and listen for the other person. There are barriers such as being afraid to hear what the other person has to say. What if there might be a criticism? We also can't listen in order to fix.

One woman I counseled use to call and would talk for an hour and half straight, I wouldn't say a word and she would still be talking. Of course she was still talking no one had ever listened to her before.

Hurts are barriers too. One time I was working with a couple who was referred to me. The woman had been married 3 times previously and an annulment needed to occur for the two to be married in the church. The man, a devout Catholic who attended 12 years of Catholic education, was a lector, and planning to study for the deaconate. He was angry about the way they were being treated. They came in and the woman was fine with all the things that needed to take place for their marriage; in fact she seemed as if she thought it was a good idea. Her marriages had been abusive and she was ready to take healthy steps. The man though, was extremely angry, a big guy too! (Images of the incredible Hulk getting mad come to mind.) He came stomping in to see me like a fire breathing dragon. He was fuming and definitely not wanting to listen to anything I might say. Finally he couldn't contain himself any longer and he blew. Like the water bellowing from a whale, he went on about the abuse that they had incurred and all they had been through. I listened and affirmed his feelings. He then calmed down and was ready to listen. So I began, "On behalf of my brothers and sisters in the church I am sorry for your hurt, will you forgive them, and will you forgive me?" You know what that man did? He wept. He needed to be listened to and have his hurt acknowledged.

Another time a mother and daughter came to see me. The mother was hurt by their tumultuous relationship and felt like her daughter was always yelling and arguing with her. She wanted me to fix the problem. I started by posing the question "What do you do when she yells?" The mother retorted back, "Well I guess I yell back." To which I asked, "Is your yelling back working?" Of course the answer was "No". I proceeded, "Then why do you keep doing it?" (I refrained from mentioning the insanity definition ... doing the same thing over and over expecting different results) and simply asked; "Would you be willing to try a different way?"

We need to provide people with different techniques', a new set of communication tools, a recipe that involves both listening, and accepting.

Opportunities for Personal Reflection and Discussion

1. What kinds of high tech tools are you using that reduce your interaction with people, perhaps limiting your opportunities for Relational Ministry?

2. How available are you by phone? How many buttons does someone calling you have to push before you might answer? Do you return phone calls and voice mail messages promptly?

3. Are you accessible in person? Is it possible for people to catch you to talk?

4. Are you alert and present when in the company of others, or are you distracted by a computer, a cell phone, or other technological devices?

5. When with your family, are you calling in to work on voicemail or on the computer? If so what can you do to be more available to your family?

6. Do you create opportunities to connect with friends and loved ones regularly?

7. Are there high tech tools you are using that could be exchanged for more personal high touch tools? How can you adapt?

CHAPTER SIX
THE SACREDNESS OF TIME IN RELATIONAL MINISTRY

"We didn't lose... we just ran out of time."
-Vince Lombardi

"Live as though you are going to die tomorrow, learn as though you are going to live forever."
-Gandhi

"Spend your time and energy in exercise of keeping spiritually fit."
- I Timothy chap 4: 7

R elational Ministry is about honoring the Sacredness of Time as a treasured commodity.

In Mike Yaconelli's book *Messy Spirituality*, he writes:

"What keeps many of us from growing is not sin but speed. Our struggle is not as much with the Bible as it is with the clock. Most people are not coming home staggering drunk. They are coming home staggering tired, exhausted, and worn out! Voices surround us, always telling us to move faster. It may be our boss, our pastor, our parents, our spouse, or even ourselves until we can't sustain. Speed has a deafening roar that drowns out the whispering voices of our soul and leaves Jesus as a diminishing speck in the rearview mirror."

We can all become too busy doing good things for God. Even church work, volunteering and community service can be obstacles when they are dividing our families. *Yaconelli writes, "Even our churches are dividing our family, emptying our faith and crushing our soul."* When this happens it's time to get out of the fast line, but how?

Time to slow down!

We realize we are not going to change the pace of the world or the dizzying speed of the cafe latte injected culture we live in. Our hope is that we will learn to set our clocks in accordance with our values. We can make small changes such as turning off the television, computer or phone? Suddenly there is time to take the kids to the park, meet a friend for coffee, or surprise your spouse by coming home from work early. Start with small changes and work from there.

What does too busy looks like:

Recently, I caught wind that a close friend had been in the hospital. I immediately called her and questioned, "Why didn't you tell me?" Her response made my heart hurt, "You are always so busy; I didn't want to bother you." OUCH!

Do you want to know what too busy looks like? It's when the people you love the most don't want to bother you in your busyness. Notice we are not talking about being available to the entire world, but rather making time for people in your schedule.

Time seems to be our most precious commodity. We all seem to be scrambling to find more of it while complaining that we don't have enough of it. But who is the keeper of our time? We are! What are we so busy doing that we do not have time for our spouses, our children, our relationships? What keeps us too busy for the things that mean the most to us? We consider money as an investment we put it in the bank. We cannot fault the bank when we do not use our money wisely and we are overdrawn. When we do not use our time wisely, we too become overdrawn. Instead of financial instability, we are risking spiritual instability of the mind, body and soul, and we end up broke.

Today's families are just plain busy! Just ask them. Nine out of ten will respond, "We are just soooo busy!" We have to take responsibility regarding our schedules. We often hear parents complain about their full time position as car pool parent transporting their children to their many activities, and yet who signed the kids up for all of these things? The parents! People are exasperated about how busy their lives are, but they are making choices to create that busyness.

How to Slow Down

In Robert Wicks' book, *Riding the Dragon*, he writes, "When beginning to feel overwhelmed we are to search our motives, fears, expectations, and habits that are causing our discomfort." Wicks emphasizes the necessity to take time to quietly and gently question ourselves and our motives in order to get clarity regarding our schedules. Once we check our motive, we are able to then make necessary changes to amend our time. Wicks uses the verbiage "Prune and prune often". He points out that if we are going to be of service to others, our ability to prune is of vital importance less we become prey to unrealistic expectations, those of other's and those of ourselves."

Looking at married couples today, we wonder how many are experiencing sacred time together. With an onslaught of families in stress and the staggering divorce rate, we know much of our time is being poorly invested. Time will not stop, but we can. We can't change time, but we can change what we do with our time. Take control of your schedule and prune in order to honor the sacredness of time spent with the people most important to you.

To appreciate the sacredness of time, we have to slow down enough to hear the whisper of Jesus.

Got Time?

There is a popular advertising campaign that says "Got Milk?" We think God might have his own campaign that says, "Got Time?" When we are too busy for God Time, we are too busy! We suggest getting out your coveted planner and scheduling in you and God Time! Put it on the calendar in pen. Noon Meeting W/ the CEO (Chief Executive Officer of me). Make time for you and God today.

Learning to slow down will be an ongoing challenge for many of us. There are ways we can encourage one another in this quest. Having an accountability partner is a way to stay honest about the way we spend our time. Once we begin to be more conscientious about our time, the easier it becomes to prune unnecessary things.

"We cannot do everything at once, but we can do something at once." Dick Van Arsdale, NBA forward

---

Too busy?

Many times we become so involved in our various tasks that we miss an opportunity to serve that was right in front of us. When we no longer see the person in front of us as anything but a distraction keeping us from our work, then it is time to reconsider who we are called to be as Disciples of Christ. Compassion does not wear a watch. The most vulnerable don't usually make appointments and the person most in need usually is not on our schedule. So how do we balance? There is a time and place for schedules. We highly recommend this for organizational purposes, but Relational Ministry also leaves room for the flexibility and freedom of the Holy Spirit. When we pray the Lord's Prayer inviting him to live in us and work through us, we must be willing to follow through with that admission. Mike Yaconelli writes "I spent so much of my time looking for God that I missed out on just being with him."

"Martha, Martha, you are anxious and worried about many things. There is need of only one thing. Mary has chosen the better part and it will not be taken from her." (Lk 10: 41-42)

Mary, the sister of Martha, piously sat at the foot of Jesus in wonder and awe. Martha, Mary's sister, was rushing about busily working and clearly frustrated with her sister's lack of help. When Martha attempted to recruit Jesus' help in scolding her sister's inactivity, Jesus responded by using Mary's example to teach Martha the importance of slowing down and just being with him. To be in the presence of God in Relational Ministry, we are challenged to slow down and just be still with Jesus.

Questions for Personal Reflection and Discussion

1. Do you feel like you are chasing time?

2. What do you need to prune?

3. How can you slow down enough to sit at the feet of Jesus? Is there a place you can go?

4. What can you do to adjust your schedule to give you more time?

5. Do people tell you how busy you are? What can you do to not be too busy?

6. Do you make regular time for you and God?

7. Can you start scheduling that in today?

CHAPTER SEVEN

LIVING YOUR MOST PASSIONATE LIFE

"The important thing about a dream is having one."
-Geoffrey F. Abert

"Vocation is not a goal to be achieved but a gift to be received. Discovering vocation does not mean scrambling toward some prize just beyond my reach but accepting the treasure of true self I already possess."
-Parker Palmer, Let Your Life Speak

"He who began a good work in you will perfect it."
-Phil 1: 6

Each of us is called to relationally minister to one another in according with our unique gifts and God's call to us. God's voice is never silent. There are times we may have difficulty hearing but fortunately we always have the Holy Spirit to guide us. There are many distractions to his voice: false expectations, misguided motives, faulty perception, low self regard, or pre-occupation with what other's think.

> "Our deepest calling is to grow into our own authentic selfhood, whether or not it conforms to some image of who we ought to be. As we do so, we will not only find the joy that every human being seeks, we will also find our path of authentic service in the world." Parker Palmer, Let Your Life Speak

We believe this process begins by first realizing the source of our power – God, and identifying our reliance in Him. Once we surrender to his will, we are ready to move forward and relationally ministry to others.

What are you passionate about? Why?

What are you passionate about? Try to set aside for a moment what you think you should be passionate about. Then, identify what you are passionate about. For many of us, this exercise is quite difficult. Many have become distant to the thought of living passionately or even dreaming. We are told what to do, what we believe, and what is meaningful. In time, we lose the ability to discern what we really think, feel or are passionate about.

"Do not grow slack in zeal." Romans 12:11

When our life in Christ becomes dull, boring, predictable and dreamless- it is time to shake things up and start to live passionately again. If we are going to *wash each other's feet,* we need to let go of complacency and societal definitions of success and re-align with the gospel message of passion. That means it is not always going to be easy, painless or predictable, but it will be full of passion!

True vocation joins self and service, as Frederick Buechner asserts when he defines vocation as "the place where your deep gladness meets the worlds' deep need. As we continue to identify our passions and God given abilities, gifts and talents, we are able to further assess what the needs are around us and how our gifts might be used to serve those needs. This journey is not usually a direct route, but it can be a scenic one if you are willing to risk.

Often in life mis-steps become the greatest gifts of all. The journey is about combining our passions with God's purpose and plan. We have the choice to sit back and watch or to step up and participate. The passionate life requires action.

For many of us, passions and talents can become entangled and confused. If we try identifying ourselves in terms of what we do or who we are, then we remove ourselves from what is most important, whose we are... God's beloved.

Who am I?

(Tammy shares)
When I was young, people would often ask me, "What are you going to be when you grow up?" I came to believe that what people did was who they were.

In high school, my perception continued to be confused and I mistakenly interpreted my self worth based on what I did. With a graduating class of 1,300, I sought my niche as a tennis player - the athletic girl with the ever-present smile regardless of what was going on in my head or heart. And it was eating me alive. Can you imagine what it is like to base the majority of your self-esteem on how successful you are on the tennis court, or how you looked in a tennis skirt?

Tennis, then, became one of the major ways in which I gauged my success and self-acceptance. When I did not measure up to the level of success I sought, I was despondent. Thus I was despondent often. I was not blessed with the natural athleticism or beauty of Maria Sharapova—but I was not willing to give up on belonging. If I played well and won, there were momentary highs and accolades that got me by for a short time. But when I lost, the defeat bled deep into my soul and I thought I had failed, not only on the tennis court, but as a human being. Pretty intense I know, but that is how I felt at the time. My self perception was faulty and it was easily rocked by the tumultuous cycle of wanting to belong.

So my search for acceptance did not get granted on the tennis court, and I was further from finding a way to meet my needs. I was out of touch with my inner need to connect with a purpose greater than myself and I kept searching through the values of the world. I don't regret those experiences, or any others for that matter and I am certainly not knocking competitive tennis. Just coming to grips with my own emptiness in searching for the meaning of life behind a wicked serve. As time goes by and I am able to reflect back on my experience, it is quite clear that the problem for me was not tennis itself—it was my attitude, my perception, and my allowing my self-worth to be defined by a game. I now see that I was not so passionate about tennis. I was passionate about belonging, and tennis was where I thought I could meet those needs. Tennis served me well. It taught me a lot about myself and about my desire to live a passionate life. Only this time, my focus is on the spiritual. Like the game of tennis, life is filled with ups and downs and wins and losses. But unlike tennis, in life, the highest score achieved is, in fact, love!

There are times many of us continue to try to make things fit, to try to look or play a part that is truly not in our heart, but that too is part of the process. Living a passionate life involves, at times going off course, or even completely getting turned around. Fortunately we can learn from every experience.

Many of us are stifled and trapped by the 'shoulds' and 'suppose to's' and 'we've always done it that way', and 'I couldn't, I'm not good enough', and so on. But if we give our-selves permission to open the door to living passionately, our lives will have renewed meaning. Living passionately, accord-ing to God's purpose and plan, in service to others is what we are made for.

Living passionately, according to God's purpose and plan, in service to others is what we were made for.

Living Passionately as Couples

Mario and Marta are marriage mentors who remind cou-ples how to dream together. They invite the couple to each have a journal and to first right down fifty of their individual dreams and goals. They encourage the participants not to limit the dreams in anyway. Next they have the couple together make a list of 50 shared dreams and goals. This exercise helps couples build their dreams together. The only thing better than living a dream, is living out that dream with someone. Mario and Marta suggest you keep the list in a place you will not lose it. Go back to it periodically recommitting to your joint pursuit of the goal and growing closer to realizing your dreams together.

We are all called to live a passionate life. Mother Teresa was an example of a passionate life lived in service to others. She washed feet for a living and we were all inspired by her example. We too have a call equally as important as Mother Teresa. What or who is your Calcutta? What is your mission or purpose? When you align yourself with God's plan, you will know. The passionate life is yours to be lived.

Relational Ministry at Work

Have you ever worked for or around someone whose style was to manipulate, intimidate, and control every move? A boss who gives tons of responsibility, but only a smidgen of authority? No matter what you did, it was never good enough? Have you experienced work situations where one employee is placed in an opposing position from another employee for the good of healthy competition? This almost always leads to disharmony and resentment and instead of accomplishing a goal of team work, the thread of trust and support is torn at from its very seam. Sometimes we are in situations where those in leadership positions find it necessary to impose their version of "constructive criticism," a vicious oxymoron if ever there was one. Criticism of any kind is destructive in its very nature. Feedback, however, can be a useful tool to help with self-growth and personal awareness. Feedback seeks ways we can improve and do better. Criticism attacks a person and has a debilitating effect. This too has a ripple effect. We tend to treat others as we ourselves have been treated. If our boss has taken a bad day out on us, our family might be in for a long night. We can change our attitude though and choose to be positive in spite of our circumstances.

"We can do no great things; only small things with great love." Mother Teresa

---

Daniel was a manager at large company. He often worked long hours, holidays and weekends. Daniel had been unhappy for sometime but continued to persevere hoping to make a difference however he could. Upper management was controlling and negative, yet Daniel tried to remain positive. Daniel did have one part of the job he enjoyed and that was his daily ping pong games with an employee named J.C.

The duo would play ping pong on their break and the conversations easily transitioned into family, faith, life and relationships. Daniel knew there was something very unique about J.C. He had a peace about him in spite of the difficult work situation that surrounded them. J.C. always had a positive attitude and a kind thing to say. He never complained. The two men became close friends and even discussed their hopes and dreams with one another. At the close of the day J.C. would wave to Daniel, and say, "I'm on your side, brother." No matter how many times Daniel heard J.C. say that, it always made him smile.

One of the dreams J.C. shared with Daniel was his desire to move to Mississippi and open a flower shop with his wife. J.C. would smile and say, "Everyone is happy to get flowers! Someday I will do it my friend, someday..."

One afternoon J.C. came to Daniel and asked if he could leave work early. He didn't give an explanation, and Daniel didn't ask for one. He just gave J.C. his blessing and sent him on his way. Soon, J.C. was coming to Daniel frequently asking for time off. He would never disclose where he was going or why he needed to leave, but Daniel knew that if J.C. needed time off, he would find a way to grant it.

This went on for quite some time and then one day J.C. came into Daniel's office and asked him if he had a minute to talk. Putting aside the work he was involved in at the time, Daniel said, "Of course I always have time for you brother." J.C.'s eyes were already filling with tears, "I want to thank you for letting me take time off whenever I asked and for never questioning me." He went on, "My wife, Sherry, has been diagnosed with cancer and it is extremely serious. They don't know how long she has to live. I've been taking her to treatment and that is why I needed the time off. She asked me to promise not to tell anyone, and I have never broken a promise to her. Daniel, I want to thank you for your support, and for allowing me to do that. I also need to tell you that I am going to retire early so I can spend every second with the woman I love, 'til death do us part.'"

Daniel had difficulty even finding the words to respond to all that J.C had just said. Instead the two men embraced. Daniel managed to muffle through his tears "I'm always on your side, brother, always."

Time passed. It has been a long and stressful day for Daniel and he stumbled up the driveway already wanting to be in bed.

He had barely settled into his recliner when the doorbell rang. Daniel tiredly staggered to the door and opened it. He was greeted by a florist holding the biggest bouquet of flowers he had ever seen. Daniel assumed the flowers were for his wife but was surprised when the card had his name on it. Curious, he opened the card, "Daniel, Greetings from The Mississippi Flower Shop! Bless you brother, I'm on your side, J.C." Once again, J.C left Daniel with a smile that rejuvenated his spirit. J.C was right. Everyone is happy to get flowers! His friend had done it. He was living his dream and that made Daniel smile even bigger.

Daniel and J.C. have kept in touch ever since, and J.C. and his wife recently celebrated another year of remission from her cancer. J.C.'s dream expanded to not only having a flower shop, but he now works with residence at a center for mentally disabled adults. J.C. gushes that he has finally found his purpose in life. Daniel also moved on to a job where he is better able to pursue his own dreams, again all in God's timing. If Daniel had not been willing to stay uncomfortable in his job, he would never have met J.C., a person who has had a profound influence on his life. The passionate life is not restricted to a life of fulfillment; rather it is an ongoing hunger to be of service to one another. It involves waiting patiently at times knowing that for everything there is a reason, even when we don't understand it until later.

Opportunities for Personal Reflection and Discussion

1. What are some of the gifts God has blessed you with?
2. What is something you are truly passionate about?
3. What gives you energy?
4. When do you feel most alive?
5. What are you doing to make a difference?
6. What are you feeling called to do?
7. What have you always dreamed of doing but haven't? What is holding you back?
8. What is something you can do today to pursue a passionate dream?

CHAPTER EIGHT

THE FOUNDATION OF RELATIONAL MINISTRY IS LOVE

"Love your neighbor as yourself."
- Leviticus 19:18a

"For the whole law can be summed up in this one command:
"Love your neighbor as yourself."
-Galatians 5:14

"Above all things have fervent love for one another, for Love
will cover a multitude of sins."
-1 Peter 4:8

The foundation of Relational Ministry is love.

The word Love can be overused or misrepresented. For example when we say we love a food or a particular TV show, that is not the kind of love we are talking about. Relational Ministry love is unconditional, interpersonal, and without judgment in regard to another person. It is given freely, not in response to anything the other person does or does not do. It is a love that remains.

Barriers to Love

As with all things in life, there are barriers, the biggest one being loving ourselves.

Ashley, a friendly, outgoing girl, who readily extended sincere praise to others, struggled desperately with her own self acceptance. She seemed to have no problem accepting others in the space they were but her most difficult critic was herself.

College was a time of transition for Ashley as it is for so many. In her efforts to find belonging and acceptance, she threw herself into many (too many) activities: sorority life, student government, athletics, councils, committees, volunteer organizations, etc. All of which proved to be quite time-consuming. Ashley soon found herself deep in a rut of over-involvement. The harder she tried, the more buried she felt. The rut was becoming a grave.

Ashley was seeking outside approval and felt she could get that through her many important roles. What she wasn't ready for was how much it was draining her. Like many of us, she was attempting to do as many good things as she could, but the busyness overcame her. Her self-esteem had been suffering so much, that she desperately tried to find some sense of who she was through these activities. Yet they failed to provide the answer.

Ashley had also put her relationship with Christ in the background. She was busy, exhausted, and not feeling very good about herself. In her mind, Christ would not want to spend time with her after her many poor choices. She wasn't feeling at all worthy of his love. Sadly, Ashley found herself in a downward spiral of eating poorly, staying up too late, struggling in her studies, and feeling guilty for the choices she found herself making. The busier she tried to keep herself, the emptier she felt.

Ashley and her best friend Kirk had grown up together. She would often turn to him and share her struggles, her loneliness, her confusion, and Kirk would listen and support her through her roller coaster of feelings. One day, Kirk called Ashley and asked if he could come by. He had something important he wanted to talk to her about. Ashley immediately thought he was coming over to lecture her, to tell her to get her act together, and she knew she deserved it. She was a mess. The doorbell rang and her heart sank knowing what she was in for. But, instead, Kirk said something very different than what Ashley was expecting.

"Ashley, you know you have been my best friend for as long as I can remember and I just needed to be sure you know something." Kirk continued, "I want you to know how much I love you and how much you mean to me." Kirk's eyes were now full of tears as he moved toward Ashley and gave her a hug and said again, "I just love you Ashley and I think you are perfect. Sometimes I worry that you don't know just how special you are. I wonder if you get how wonderful you are just because of who you are, not by what you do." Ashley looked at Kirk with confusion. "Kirk, this has been the lowest point in my life. I am a mess, and I don't understand what you see." He looked into her eyes as he held her, tears now cascading down her cheeks and said, "Ashley, I see the same thing I have always seen- your beautiful heart."

What Kirk helped Ashley see was how Christ loves her- uncon-ditionally, not because we deserve it, not when we are perfect, just because he does - always. He loves us through our messiness, through our fumbling, our failings, and our poor choices. He looks past our imperfections and sees our heart, just as Kirk reflected to Ashley.

Ashley found what was missing in her life. It wasn't activities, and it wasn't even Kirk, although he was a god-send to her. The answer was Ashley's relationship with Christ, and with herself. When she learned to accept herself, not as the successful superwoman, but as the hurting child of God, she found the peace she had been searching for. Kirk's love for Ashley and belief in her even when she did not believe in herself helped her to start making better choices, including saying no to over-activity. Something many of us struggle with.

Ashley says that when she was at her lowest, God gave her his greatest. Christ loves us where we are and he asks us to love each other in the same way.

The subtitle to Mike Yaconelli's book *Messy Spirituality* is "*God's Annoying Love for Imperfect People*". How true! Although we can't begin to understand the depths of Christ's love for us, we long to embrace his love and return it. We can share in it by the way we relationally minister to each other.

Christ gives us a model of this unconditional acceptance of ourselves and others, and he extends to us an invitation to walk in his ways. Ashley accepted Kirk's love, although she could have rejected it. Christ gives each of us the same invitation, which we can likewise accept or reject. We can deny our own goodness, and we can refuse to reflect the goodness of others—or we can turn toward Christ, accept his love, and love one another in response to his call.

Made in the Image of God

Some people stay stuck in the rut of believing the lies of this world: that we are not good enough, that we are junk. Fr. Gale jokes, "Hey, I drive a Volkswagen and even they have recalls from time to time. I think if God made a mistake he would want to recall it and fix it, but that's not what God has done. He has made all of us in his image and likeness, and if we believe in his goodness, we are called to believe in our own goodness as well. God doesn't limit himself; we do."

"God made man in his image and likeness, and unfortunately man returned the favor."

God made man in his image and likeness, and unfortunately we returned the favor. But our ways are not God's ways, even when we try to make them so. It won't work. Whenever we continue to beat up on ourselves, it is important to remember that those messages are not from God. God only makes masterpieces, not junk. When we question our goodness, we are questioning his masterpiece.

God also gives us the gift of special people in our lives— like Kirk was to Ashley— and Sarah was to Fr. Gale who reflect this love back to us. God's love is like a circle. God is love, he loves us, we in turn learn to love ourselves, and then we are able to love others in the way God first loved us.

Love is Acceptance

(Fr. Gale Shares)

I spent many years of my life searching for a definition of love. In the first letter of John, Chapter 4, verse 8, John says, "God is love."

If I am going to define love, then I have to be able to place my definition in the context of God, and that definition should make sense. After many years of searching for the right phrase, I have settled on one that fits that requirement: Love is acceptance.

God is acceptance. He accepts me for who I am. He invites me to grow, but he accepts me for the beautiful person he created. God is acceptance. Love is acceptance.

Therefore, love is not a feeling. It is a decision I have control over. I can decide to love even when I am not feeling it. I can decide to love regardless of how I feel at any particular moment.

When I wake up in the morning, I can decide to be a loving person even though I don't feel loving (which is quite often the case, as I am not a morning person). I can reach out to others, be cheerful, and be happy. Since feelings tend to follow actions, if I act in a loving way, I can begin to have feelings of love or at least closeness to others.

Love is a decision, and we are called to make that decision daily.

Love is a decision

Love is a decision, a choice. God chose to love us into existence, and we are called to continue that act of creation, to share in that act of creation, by loving each person we come in contact with. This is the relational ministry challenge we are called to live out each day, thereby choosing love for each other.

Opportunities for Personal Reflection and Discussion

1. When have you been shown love even when you felt unworthy?

5. Who is someone you choose to love today unconditionally?

6. What does your most significant love relationship look like?

7. Who has loved you with the love of Jesus?

8. Can you accept another's love for you in spite of your imperfections?

9. Can you accept God's love for you even in your messiness?

10. How do you see your love relationship with Jesus today?

11. Is there anything you want to say to him? Write him now.

CHAPTER NINE
LIVING AUTHENTIC RELATIONAL MINISTRY

"Whatever the circumstance, whatever the status of our lives, God is present—waiting for us to discover him, waiting for us to learn from him in the shadows as well as the light."
-Mike Yaconelli, Dangerous Wonder

"What good is it, my brothers, if someone says he has faith but does not have works? What if a brother or sister has nothing to wear and has no food for the day and one of you says, "Go in peace, keep warm and eat well," but you do not give them the necessities of the body, what good is it? So also faith of itself, if it does not have works, is dead."
-James 2:14-17

"My beloved friend let us continue to love each other since love comes from God. Everyone who loves is born of God and experiences a relationship with God."
-1 John 4:7-8

Relational Ministry is striving to live authentically in all areas of our life. It is learning to trust ourselves and others as we begin to open up honestly. When we are able to reveal our true selves by sharing our thoughts and feelings and by listening to another in the same way, we are experiencing authentic Relational Ministry. Revealing ourselves and our feelings can be difficult as it opens us up to being vulnerable to another person. Many of us have become experts at covering up our feelings and stuffing them back into our subconscious. We even attempt to anesthetize them in various ways: Alcohol, Sleep, TV, The Internet, Work, Volunteering, Eating, Exercising, Spending, Religiosity or any number of escapes that people turn to in trying to numb the pain. What are we running from? It's usually our feelings.

Running from Feelings

Elijah was a member of the church youth group. His mom, Renee, was extremely religious and would see to it that Elijah was signed up for every youth event. Renee was at church so much, she often would be mistaken for a member of the staff. Elijah had a disability that required him to walk with crutches, and sometimes he would need a wheelchair when he became extremely fatigued. There was a youth trip coming up and Renee was the first one to sign up Elijah. The youth minister, Pam, knew that the event would require a lot of walking, so there would come a time Elijah would need to use the wheelchair. Pam always looked forward to the special time she had with Elijah.

The challenges that Elijah faced physically never diminished his spirit or his sense of humor, and he was a joy to be with. Elijah felt safe with Pam and the two had a special connection. During the trip while Pam was pushing Elijah in his wheelchair, he started to share with her some deep questions and feelings. Pam listened to Elijah and then she encouraged him to talk to his mom about what he had shared. Pam understands the importance of family communication. Elijah quickly responded, "I can't talk to my mom about anything. She doesn't have time for me. In fact, she doesn't have room in her heart for anyone but God. That's all she cares about—spending time at church and praying. I just get in her way."

Pam's heart sank. She knew that Elijah's mom would have been despondent to hear his thoughts. Later, Pam learned that Elijah's mom and dad were divorcing. She then was able to better understand why his mom had resorted to the familiarity and comfort of religion for solace. It also revealed that even religion can be used by some as a place to hide, or escape, anything to help dull the pain. Religion itself is not a negative thing. It can be a wonderful way to worship in a community, however even religion, when it becomes a means by which families are separated, can be harmful. Religiosity is not the same thing as spirituality.

Today Elijah is not affiliated with any organized religion which is understandable given his experience. At the time Renee was unable to see her own blind spot concerning Elijah's true need- the need for his mom.

We all have our blind spots. Being able to recognize our own blind spots is a huge step in self awareness. Being willing to allow the feedback from another person (such as a mentor) to illuminate our blind spots takes wisdom and humility. When we are more in touch with our shadows, defects and blind spots, we learn to recognize the warning signs and move into redemptive action.

As long as we continue to hide, project and masquerade our imperfections, we will continue to stay stuck in spiritual blindness. When we learn to acknowledge our authentic self, we realize that it is the people we share our shadow side with that we feel the closest to. Relational Ministry is about loving the shadow and the light. It is about loving the PTA President and the prostitute, the Airline Pilot and the hitch hiker, the doctor and the drug dealer. We are all broken disciples. The only real cure starts with the healing power of love.

Robert Wicks, in his book *Riding the Dragon*, talks eloquently about the dark and shadow sides of his journey and refers to them as his basement experiences. Not many of us like going into the dark, cold, gloomy basement. The feelings that usually co-exist there can be painfully immobilizing. But what if we could accept our basement experience as a necessary part of our spiritual journey? What if we can learn to embrace such opportunities as spiritual growth? After all if we didn't ever descend into the darkness of the basement, we wouldn't be able to appreciate the full extent of the light. We all have basement experiences, some of us more frequently than others. Through it all, we can continue to help one another journey toward the light, stronger, more capable and more compassionate.

Embracing our Shadow

We don't usually want to acknowledge our own shadow sides having to accept how we might have acted inappropriately, or hurt another. It is so much easier to blame and project what someone else did without wanting to look at our part.

Relational Ministry is about taking responsibility for our part, and not anyone else's. What we do, what we say, how we respond are the focus. Not looking at another person's part, but simply focusing on our part. We are not victims, we are participants. We are not powerless, we are empowering. Until we learn to take responsibility for our actions, we will forever be delusional about our own inadequacies. When we start taking responsibility for our own actions, we release the other person. Let them handle their side of the street. Relational ministry is not about blaming, shaming, or condemning another. It is about accepting others as they are and trying to always improve ourselves.

One way we can take responsibility for our own actions is to allow feedback from others. We are not suggesting you take feedback from everyone. Not everyone will be healthy enough to offer you sound feedback. When you do trust the source, filter in feedback as if it were flour being poured through a sifter. Some will stick and some won't. Take what you like and leave the rest. Use the information to help you grow and then let it go. Remember healthy people are able to give feedback; unhealthy people rely on criticism. Keep that in mind when choosing who you will trust for feedback.

There are many of us who are too frightened to admit, confess, or acknowledge our true selves to another person. Jesus told us to confess our sins to one another. In program, there is a saying: "We are only as sick as our secrets." When we let go of fear and trust another person with our true self, spiritual healing can be realized.

Once we embrace our whole self, even our defects, we can see the gifts that all of our experiences offer, even the bad ones. When everything in life is seen as a teachable moment, life takes on a whole new kaleidoscope of possibilities.

We have established that God makes no mistakes. We all have shadows and we can grow stronger through them. What a wonderful freedom it is to let go of the need to be perfect! We are striving for progress not perfection. When we get in touch with our authentic self and embrace it, then we are able to let others in, to trust one another and be honest. We then open ourselves up for deeper friendships and life-changing relationships where growth is constant. Until we reveal our weaknesses, our struggles, and our imperfections, we are not allowing others to really know us. The more honest we become with ourselves and others, the deeper we are able to connect in our relationships.

Assuming Good Faith

Assume good faith means to resist the temptation to get in another person's head and pretend to know what they are thinking. We are quick to jump to conclusions, hearsay, gossip or something someone says out of context and exaggerate it in our head. When we take the attitude of assuming good faith, we give the person the benefit of the doubt of doing the best they can with who they are and what we don't know. We are quick to react with hurt (anger turned inward), and then we let our pride, ego, and defensiveness take over rather than assuming good faith on the part of the other.

While it is important to feel our feelings, including our hurts, it is also important to allow others to be who they are, accept where they are, and surrender the need to fix them. Perhaps the other person doesn't have the tools of communication necessary to engage a healthy dialogue. Perhaps because of life events and unhealed hurts, he or she is reacting out of fear. What if we learn to love them anyway? Love them and accept them as they are? Isn't this what Jesus asks of us when he says to 'Wash Each Other's Feet.'

At the core of Relational Ministry is the call to act in love. If we truly love our neighbor as ourselves, if we believe God is love and that he is in charge, we will then be able to give our lives over to him and he will help us turn our deficits into assets, and our weaknesses into strengths. We can then trust, self-disclose and open ourselves up to others.

Imprints on our Heart

Think of a person as soft warm wax. It can be easily molded and formed. When a person touches the wax, imprints are left on it. Some are gentle and delicate; others rough and forceful. All of them make up the form. We are all like soft wax when we are children. Our entire lives others' are leaving their imprints on us. In time the wax hardens and the form has taken shape. What does your wax figure look like?

When we love, we will always be vulnerable to the imprints of others. We also have to take responsibility for the great amount of imprinting we ourselves do. We have the awesome ability to influence others, positively or negatively. If the imprints we have received have led us to see ourselves as good and lovable, we will reflect that to others. If we believe otherwise, that will be reflected as well.

The hope remains in that the hardened wax can be warmed again, softened by the love of another, and continuously reshaped. Remember that each of us is a work in progress. Just as that hardened wax can be softened, so too can our hearts. As always, love resides at the heart of Relational Ministry, a love that can move mountains and open the heart to the love of God and others.

Questions for Personal Reflection and Discussion

1. What barriers are preventing you from living your most authentic life?

2. What are your blind spots?

3. Do you have someone you can honestly confess to?

4. Do you believe you are completely loved in spite of your shadow side?

5. What would your candle look like?

6. What fears keep you from revealing your true self?

7. How can you overcome those fears?

8. Are you willing to risk being vulnerable and let someone in? Who? What action step can you take today?

9. Who could you reach out to who might need your unconditional acceptance today?

CHAPTER TEN
THE FAMILY AS THE WELLSPRING OF RELATIONAL MINISTRY

*"Put on, then, as God's chosen ones, holy and beloved, heartfelt compassion, kindness, humility, gentleness, and patience, bearing with one another and forgiving one another ... **and over all these put on love, that is, the bond of perfection.** And let the peace of Christ control your hearts, the peace into which you were also called in one body."*
— Col. 3:12-15

"You have the power to lift each other up to the gates of heaven, or the power to cast each other into the depths of hell."

To have a better spouse- be a better spouse!

Ask not, What can my spouse do for me- but, What can I do for my spouse.

Empathy in Marriage

*I*t had been a long week for Paula. She was physically and emotionally exhausted. Her husband Brian walked in the door from a business trip and all she could do was manage a forced hello from the kitchen. Brian walked over to his wife and greeted her with a kiss sensing her frustration. Paula got a little tense thinking he better not even think about it- I am exhausted! Then Brian wrapped his arms around her and presented her with a gift box that was wrapped with a red bow. She hesitated to open it a little irritated he would think that his long absence would easily be overlooked with a present. She tried to pretend she was grateful, but Brian could see through her façade and smiled knowing she might soon feel like she was understood more than she thought. Inside was a gift certificate for a day at a spa, a luxury Paula had only dreamed about.

Brian had written a note inside "Enjoy your day, you deserve to be pampered! I'm so sorry I have been gone so long. Thank you for all you do. I appreciate you so much. I love you Angel, Brian." Paula burst into tears and wrapped her arms around Brian, falling into him and letting her hold her. He really did understand, she thought. The following day Paula went to the spa and Brian and the kids cleaned the house, went to the store and made Paula dinner. She returned a new woman, refreshed more internally than externally. She had gotten a much needed break and was ready to give herself to her family once again now that she had her own pitcher filled back up. What Brian figured out, that many of us miss, is that he was able to consider Paula's needs before his own. Instead of coming home expecting to be waited

105

on after a hard week of working out of town, Brian chose to focus on Paula's needs. In return Paula became much more sensitive to Brian's needs. The giving became reciprocal and the couple was able to enjoy their relationship even in the midst everyday stress.

Love can be worked at in many ways - Gary Chapman's book, *Love Languages,* is a great book for couples to read together. The book helps couples understand that most times we love another person in the way we want to be loved. When the reality is their love language may be quite different and what they need is something different entirely. Brian figured out Paula's love language and the couple was able to grow together in harmony.

The First Couple

> "God created man in His image; male and female. God blessed them, saying to them; "Be fruitful and multiply; fill the earth and subdue it." (Gn 1:27-28)

God knew that man did not want to be alone. He knew we needed each other and therefore created a couple—and Relational Ministry was born.

This first couple, Adam and Eve in the Genesis story, were presented with the opportunity to reflect back each other's goodness. If it were only Adam (man) or only Eve (woman), there would be no one to reflect back, thus no Relational Ministry.

Unfortunately, so the story goes, Adam and Eve had relationship issues like the rest of us, and consequently they blamed each other. "She made me do it Lord!" "He brought me to the tree." Then they judged themselves unworthy of the goodness that was God's creation and they fell into relationship rockiness. Like Adam and Eve, we, too, fall into the temptation of imposing negative judgments on ourselves, our partner, and our creator. We might get in touch with a negative thought, which gives birth to negative feelings, which over time spirals into a negative behavior, and the cycle of dysfunction continues.

There is hope. We can transform our thinking and behaving into reflecting back our innate goodness and that of others. The person who is fully aware of the shadow side and sets that aside to instead focus on the gifts, assets, and internal beauty of each person is the hope of Relational Ministry. All relationships take time, nurturing, selfless giving, and unconditional love. Relational Ministry in marriage is a sacred union that brings us together with another person and our creator as one. This is the most intimate relationship possible, so much so that it is from that relationship that new life is created.

Marriage as Cause for Celebration.

The family is dedicated to love, belonging, and nurturing as its primary function. It is the medium through which our first foundation is laid. The family is the institution which first teaches us how to survive and thrive in the world. A person's lessons regarding values, virtues, and philosophies are first introduced in their family system, whatever that looked like. The family has a profound responsibility and impact on a child's first relationships and can greatly influence the way in which they see the world. Thus it is the ultimate testing ground for Relational Ministry.

Family life today is more diverse than ever. There is, however, a commonality that all families share—relationship. Whether it is a healthy or dysfunctional relationship, we are all participants. Some of us came away from those family relationships with mostly positive memories and effective tools to live our lives. Others walk away with what they want to do differently. The commonality is that we all want to be loved, cared for, and accepted and our families are where we first experience these desires. Jesus' first miracle was changing water into wine at the wedding feast at Cana. Marriage can definitely be a great cause for celebration.

Love as Grounds for Marriage

There is a joke that says any couple married longer than twenty-four hours can probably find grounds for divorce. But what if we started with turning that around and finding grounds for marriage? It can be discouraging to watch how quickly some married couples lose sight of the gift their presence was to each other. When things start falling apart and the sense of joy and celebration is lost, couples lose touch with the grounds for marriage, which is based on unconditional love! We need to plant seeds of joy and celebration not only at the beginning of our married life but throughout, and never stop nurturing them. If we don't nurture a plant with water and sunshine, it will die. The day we stop nurturing our marriages they too are at the same risk.

The Sacrament of Marriage

Fr. Gale tells couples in his relationship workshops and counseling, "You have the power to lift each other up to the gates of heaven, but you also have the power to cast each other into the depths of hell."

"You have the power to lift each other up to the gates of heaven, but you also have the power to cast each other into the depths of hell."

He tells couples to "lift up your love on a regular basis." He challenges couples to take their responsibility to do so seriously and use it honorably. Isn't that our call? To treat all our brothers and sisters in this way? To constantly reflect back each other's goodness? And if this is so, how much more should we lift up the one we are called to be with 'til death do us part'?

Jesus put at the center of the family the couple relationship. It is the foundation from which all other relationships develop. Is there any more intimate relationship two people can share than as a married couple? And yet the institution designed to unite two people in love is the institution that can also be the most challenging in living out the Relational Ministry principles we have discussed.

What is this power that married couples have at their disposal? It is, of course, the power of love. Love is indeed a powerful force, one capable of moving mountains, bridging the widest chasm, and healing the deepest wound, and when it is missing, the heart is torn asunder.

Fr. Gale emphasizes that the sacrament is called marriage, not parenthood. Children are welcome members—to an already existing family, but they are not meant to be the center of the family system. When they are put there, the married couple's relationship becomes secondary and therefore at risk.

The love of the sacramental couple has great power, a power with far-reaching influence. Think of a calm clear pond as a stone is tossed into the center, the ripple effect continuing far beyond the point of impact. The same is true for the married couple's impact on the world around them.

Date Your Mate!

How can we nurture the sacrament of marriage? First of all, we need to make the time! Couples should have a minimum of 15 minutes alone daily, an evening every weekend, and a vacation getaway once a year for just the couple. These are essential.

Our culture has forced us to deal with the question of why so many marriages are in disrepair, why the divorce rate is at an all-time high, why more and more couples are reporting increased dissatisfaction in their marriage relationship. Why indeed? Time and time again, the answer is—time.

Couple time is the important missing ingredient. Time together to laugh, play, pray, communicate, and invest in one another. If someone else is getting the best of your time, your marriage partner only gets the leftover scraps, and the relationship will begin to look like leftovers as well. Once the couple makes the commitment to invest time, energy, and nourish the relationship, new joy will be found.

Couple time should not be a choice; it should be a mandate. Seatbelts protect people's lives as they travel by car. Couple time protects married couple's hearts in the same way. Without it, the seatbelt or the date, the consequence can be life-threatening, whether it is a person or a relationship.

That weekly date night is a challenge for many. We can come up with any number of excuses for putting it off—we'll get to it when the children are older, when we're not quite so busy at work, when we can find more time or money.

There is a common misconception that there will be time for the couple relationship once the kids are grown and gone. The reality is that if you don't invest in the relationship now, there might not be anything left later.

The natural course of life is that the kids grow up and ultimately leave, creating their own family unit. Outside of the revolving-door syndrome that some empty nesters experience, there does come a time when the kids are gone and the couple is left staring at each other, wondering where all the years have gone. When they look into each other's eyes, will they see a familiar and trusted friend, or just a stranger with more wrinkles? Children are meant to leave the nest; they were created with that in mind. We give them roots and wings and set them free. But marriage partners are meant to stay and grow together in the nest. If we are too busy to nurture the marriage relationship now, there will be consequences later.

There is much truth to the saying 'the greatest gift a father can give his children is to love their mother, and the greatest gift a mother could give her children is to love their father.' Showing your children that you are committed to investing in your couple relationship reinforces security in them. The couple is modeling how to nurture the most significant love relationship. What we model is most often imitated. Is the relationship you have with your spouse the same you would want for your children? If not, what can you do to improve your relationship?

New Hope

We believe that we have reached a unique period in history, one in which we see the potential for marriage providing the exemplar of how to minister to one another relationally. With God's help, and our own committed efforts, we may very well be on the brink of experiencing the phenomenal power of Relational Ministry in marriage.

(Fr. Gale Shares)

My parents got married in 1927. The reason they got married was for survival, not intimacy. The skills needed for success in marriage back then were simple—providing, protecting, and educating. My father was the provider and protector, and my mother was the educator. Children were considered a financial asset to the family, especially male children. If a couple achieved intimacy, it was a nice plus, but basically the couple was satisfied if they just "got along."

Today we see clear signs of a changing paradigm of marriage. Today when a couple gets married, their goal is to be each other's best friend. They demand intimacy as the core of their relationship, so the requisite skills have changed. We're no longer looking for providing, protecting, and educating only. Now we seek and desire communication, conflict resolution, healing, empowerment and intimacy.

Only about five to seven percent of married couples today achieve this goal consistently, but that five to seven percent, as low as it may seem, is much greater than at any previous time in the history of the human race. I believe that percent will continue to increase in the coming years, and marriage will become the leading institution in teaching communities about belonging, what it means to be in relationship, and how we are called to minister to each other daily. Starting with married couples, then moving out to all interpersonal relationships, we will find ourselves "washing each other's feet" as we listen to each other, forgive each other, and reflect back each other's goodness."

It's easy to fall back into taking each other for granted and losing the joy of being one. We will all need to continuously encourage each other to make these concepts alive in our relationships. We will need to be reminded of what it means to cherish each other, as we are called to practice these virtues throughout our lives. We also have a responsibility to support, encourage and lift up other married relationships. Remember we are not asked to go through anything alone, not even our marriages. Find a support system today.

Opposites Attract

One of the common challenges that couples encounter in marriage comes after the initial attraction wears off. Over time, the appreciation for differences that once attracted them toward each other begins to fade, and the couple gets down to the business of married life. That cute thing the other person did or said which initially attracted them now becomes a little irritating. If the couple does not make the time to reconnect, the irritation could grow into something a whole lot bigger.

The different personalities that have come together are meant to make a stronger whole. One union formed from the best traits of two people who are united in love. We are drawn to those who fill our gaps and allow us to get in touch with unrealized parts of our own personality. These traits complement one another and the couple grows together.

Expectations in Marriage

Adding to the equation of different personalities, each of us enters marriage with a different understanding of what a husband is supposed to be and what a wife is supposed to be. Perceptions developed through our family of origin and life. These expectations are played out daily in the marriage relationship. Making time to regularly discuss and communicate each other's expectations is an important exercise in relational ministry.

Amy and Blake were excited to be celebrating their first Christmas together as a married couple — not he with his family and she with hers, but together now as one family. But the excitement quickly faded into marital conflict, a conflict stemming from expectations of rituals and traditions.

Blake had always opened presents on Christmas morning; Amy's family had always opened presents on Christmas Eve. These were important traditions to both of them and neither wanted to change or even compromise on his or her treasured customs. After all, that is the way their family had always done it, of course making it the right way to do it, as if there were such a thing.

So on Christmas Eve, tensions started mounting; Amy was catching up on wrapping in the back room when Blake came in to see what she was doing. To which Amy replied, "I am wrapping your family's Christmas presents." Blake took one look at the packages and said, "My family doesn't even wrap presents, and they definitely wouldn't put all those frilly bows on them."

By now, Amy was beyond compassion and she retorted back, "Well mine does, and I can decorate the packages any way I want!" Blake, failing to grasp the importance of letting things be, fired back, "Well you can put as many stupid bows as you want on your family's presents, but not on the presents we are giving to my family." Blake then proceeded to de-bow the packages for his family.

Amy, could not hold it in any longer and she ran out of the room and into the bedroom, where she slammed the door, and buried her head in her pillow, sobbing, while wondering why she had married this man. Fortunately, Blake recalled something he had heard in their marriage preparation classes—about choosing your battles. He humbled himself, went into the bedroom, and apologized to Amy. He asked her to forgive him and if together they could go and finish decorating all of the packages-with as many bows as she wanted. When Amy looked up from the pillow she saw that Blake had stuck bows all over his head and she immediately began to laugh. Laughter sometimes really is the best medicine.

Sharing Our Stories

One helpful approach to strengthening our marriage is to be connected to other married couples, specifically couples who serve as mentors. The mentor couple can offer hope by revealing their own experiences, things they have encountered, overcome, and journeyed through, both their challenges and their victories. Sharing our stories is a great way to encourage one another in marriage. We are not alone, despite how we can feel at times.

Prayer groups, classes, books, seminars, community involvement, retreats, mentors,—all provide the opportunity for continued marriage enrichment. When we risk, share, open up, and disclose our fears and challenges, we are able to grow together. If we keep to ourselves we risk loneliness, isolation and increasing despair.

When it Doesn't Work Out

Angie recalls the day her parents took her aside to tell her that some family friends were getting a divorce. She recalls the confusion and pain that engulfed her. She felt like her safe little world had just been knocked off its axis, and she began to question the foundation of her own family unit. Would her parents get a divorce too? She was only eight years old.

Sometimes, the reality is that it doesn't work out. For whatever reason people find themselves in the situation thinking, "This was not suppose to happen to me." Many of us have experienced the sadness or disbelief upon discovering that a couple we've known is getting divorced. Mixed with that sadness is our own frustration and guilt: How could I have helped? Was I too busy to see the signs? Did I fail to offer support?

When a couple divorces, it affects all of us. What can we do? We can start by thinking abut how we can reach out to them, providing the support they will still need? Among the challenges experienced by divorcing couples are friends pulling away, feelings of loneliness and abandonment, the fear of starting all over again, the guilt surrounding the question of what could have been done to salvage the marriage, financial insecurity, and more. We've heard quite a few people over the years confiding that they thought their church community would be a place where they would receive support, but what they found instead was judgment.

What if instead of pointing fingers at others, we could stop and ask, "What can I do to help?" Until we walk in another's shoes, we will never fully understand their experience. At this difficult time in a couple's life, we are called to listen, love and support them; they don't need a judge, they need a friend.

The Key

We have mentioned several factors that influence the couple relationship: differences in family background, variations in personality styles, different understandings of roles, and the challenge of a culture increasingly unsupportive of married life. All of which can lead to a sense of overwhelming discouragement.

When we are able to set aside the frustrations of living together, we begin to work on relating to each other in spite of our differences. What if the couple could exchange keys like they did wedding vows, reminding them of the trust they allowed into their heart through that other person. This key opens a place where dirt and messiness are exposed and the person is made vulnerable revealing the imperfections we try so hard to conceal.

Presenting this key to the other person can continue to keep the lines of communication open. The key is communication and what it opens up is a bridge to the heart. Go to God for help. He gave you one another and will help you throughout your lives together. We don't recommend trying to do it without him!

Day to Day

Let's see how this key, which is heart-to-heart communication, works in the day-to-day lives of a married couple. If it sounds familiar, then find comfort in knowing you are not alone.

Courtney and Kyle are a beautiful young couple caught up, like most of us, in a whirlwind of busyness—jobs, social activities, volunteering, church, school and community commitments, all while shuttling the kids back and forth to school, soccer games, dance class, basketball practice, music lessons and so on.

One day, Courtney arrived home after a long day, her car packed with groceries she had just picked up and was elated to find Kyle's car parked in the driveway, much earlier than his return time. Her first reaction was joy, and she exclaimed to the kids, "Daddy's home." The kids joined in with excitement with their own chorus of "Daddy's home, Daddy's home!"

Entering the house, Courtney found Kyle in his familiar spot, lounging in the recliner in front of the TV, remote control firmly in hand. "Hi, Sweetie," she exclaimed, grocery bag in one arm, youngest child in the other. "We're surprised and glad to see you home from work early." Thinking of the grocery packages in the car and the three needy kids all wanting attention, she continued, "Hey, Babe, can you give me a hand?" Kyle, in a very different place entirely and clearly annoyed by this intrusion on his quiet time, mumbled, "Sure, just give me a few minutes. This is almost over."

Courtney felt a surge of irritation as she thought to herself, "I wish I had a few minutes!" and then continued unloading the groceries and children from the car by herself. The kids, overjoyed to see Daddy, came bouncing in and onto daddy's lap. "Daddy, Daddy, you're home, I made a picture today, I played outside, we went to the store, Mommy got us a treat, I have a new Band-Aid . . ." Kyle, torn between the joy of experiencing his children leaping into his arms and his desire for those few minutes of solitude called out to Courtney, with just a hint of annoyance, "Can you grab the kids? This is almost over."

The children, picking up on their father's disinterest and growing agitation, sought out the kitchen where they could help their mom, for whom stress and agitation had by now replaced the earlier joy and excitement.

"Mommy, can we help?" they pleaded, only to be met with a response similar to that of dad's. "Girls, can you just go play in your room for a minute? Mommy really needs to get this done quickly right

now." *The kids trundled off to their rooms; the pure joy that had once overflowed spontaneously in their legs and hearts dampened a bit by Mom's and Dad's busyness.*

Some fifteen minutes into the next TV show—what happened to the "just few more minutes?—Kyle, was alerted that something was amiss due to the banging of pots, pans, cabinets and doors in the kitchen. He turned off the TV and sought out Courtney, hoping to make amends before all was lost. But it was too late, and the cold shoulder was all that greeted him.

"What's wrong?" he asked.

"Nothing, nothing at all!" was her retort. Kyle persisted until she finally unleashed.

"You know exactly what's wrong!" She yelled.

"No, I don't. I can't read your mind. You are always mad about something! What did I do this time?" He shouted back.

"If only you would make time for the girls. They just wanted a minute of your attention. Megan told me that Phil reads to his daughter for an hour every night!" Courtney exclaimed.

"Well, maybe you should have married Phil." Kyle fired back.
"Well, maybe I should have!" and so it went.

Sometimes we can't seem to stop the words from spewing out of our mouths. Out of our hurt and discouragement, we criticize, we blame, and we belittle, using the same words over and over again and, no doubt, expecting them to effect a change that has eluded us so many times before. Soon, it is no longer about our frustration; it is about our survival. We all have the basic human needs of —respect, partnership, and love. But we have to learn ways to get out of the spiral of destructive dialogue.

Let's start with Courtney. A tired wife and mom who desperately needs a break, she feels overwhelmed. Courtney feels like all she does all day is clean up after the kids, who only mess it all up again, so why bother? Is this what she went to school to get her degree for? Her husband comes home to find a messy house and wonders aloud what she did all day. Courtney is feeling lonely. An extrovert, she craves adult interaction and never seems to find enough opportunities for it.

Her best friend was just made partner at the law firm they once worked at together. The woman she met at the grocery store today went on and on about her wonderful husband and how much he helps her. He just surprised her with a weekend getaway to a bed and breakfast, just to thank her for all she does for their family and to let her know how much he appreciates her. Courtney wonders if it will ever get better.

And what about Kyle? He is working sixty-plus hours a week. He can't seem to catch up; the workload just gets heavier and heavier. A co-worker just got laid off, and he worries about his own job security, while wondering how he will fill the gap of one less employee. Kyle has a wife and three daughters—and they are expensive! The bills just keep coming in, and he feels completely buried. He has lunch with a co-worker who talks about the golf game he played this past weekend, and Kyle can't remember the last time he did something for fun. An introvert, he secretly longs for an escape, a place to be alone and just rest for a bit. He wonders if it will ever get better.

And what about the children? You can imagine what kinds of thoughts are playing through their minds. We return to what we stated earlier: The best way to build a child's sense of security is for his father to love his mother and his mother to love his father. All the parenting books that Courtney and Kyle have read will be of little value until the children experience their treating each other in a loving manner. Children are excellent perceivers.

Courtney and Kyle need a break, a date night, time together to talk, reconnect and focus on their primary relationship—each other. Here are six tools to help:

1. Schedule regular date nights
In addition to the daily special couple time, and annual vacations, Courtney and Kyle would benefit from regular date

nights where they can renew their relationship. They need to connect with a special time that is not devoted to talking about the kids, which can sometimes be a diversion from the couple's communication. Part of the time can be used for problem solving as well. This allows the couple to experience time together—to talk, to play, to pray and to touch, all critical components of the marriage relationship.

2. Make compromises and help each other.

Helping one another is essential to keeping peace. Marriage is about co-partnership. Finding ways to work as a team creates a peaceful home environment and also serves as a good model for young eyes that are watching and learning. A shared model of teamwork is effective.

3. Honor Differences

Remember that opposites attract. Allow that person to be who he or she is, and make every effort to accept and honor that person's attribute. Let go of expectations, and celebrate the balance of opposites. What might seem like an obstacle at times, is also an asset, as the differing strengths come together to complement the whole.

4. When you have the choice to be right or kind – be kind!

We respect the other person when we treat them with kindness. Kind communication is often expressed as "I statements," which serve the purpose of allowing us to take ownership of feelings, and communicate without blame. Remember how we say things make a big difference.

The "you" approach blames and hardly makes the other person want to help. The "I" approach allows the person to participate in a respectful manner and lays out the specific request of what would be helpful. 'You' verbiage, such as 'You always' or 'You never', are quick ways to put the other person on the defensive. One approach leads to hurt, the other to healing.

5. Let go of the power-struggle

There is the old saying that there are two words that make a marriage work- "Yes Dear". The reality is when we stop the power struggle; we can find a common ground. One grandmother says "Quit trying to make your husband into a wife. He's a dad, not a mom." Wise words! When we can accept the gifts the other person has and let go of the expectation of doing things "My Way", peace and harmony can co-exist!

6. Take a time-out

Sometimes the wisest approach to a disagreement is to disengage. There is often new perspective after a brisk walk, a good night sleep or quiet time in prayers. You may have heard that couples should never let the sun set on an argument, which often results in couples fighting throughout the night. If you're arguing and you sense things are not going well, take a time out. (Think about why kids are asked to take a time out—to calm down, to reflect, to think about what they did, not what someone else did.) Get some rest - you might be fighting in fact because you are overtired.

Continuing an argument in the expectation that it will somehow be resolved amid growing tempers can cause more harm than good. One person may simply give in to the other with only hard feelings resulting. This scenario would leave one person as winner and one as a loser. Fr. Gale often remarks in his seminars, who wants to be married to a loser? Not a healthy way to view your couple relationship. If it's not a win/win- it is a loss for all.

When we extend ourselves to meet the needs of another, even placing the other's needs before our own, we experience the blessings of relational ministry in the most intimate sense. To have a better spouse- remember to be a better spouse! It is in giving that we receive!

Opportunities for Personal Reflection and Discussion

1. What are some of the ideas you established about marriage when you were growing up?

2. What expectations from your family of origin have you kept with you?

3. How do members of your community reach out to support marriage relationships?

4. Is there something you could do to improve your relationship?

5. What resentment do you need to let go of to draw closer to your significant other?

6. What tools will you incorporate into your marriage relationship today? Date night? Vacation? 15 minutes?

7. Is there another married couple that you know who could benefit from your support? What can you do to encourage them?

Chapter Eleven

Feeling Our Feelings

"It takes courage to grow up and become who you really are."
- e. e. Cummings

"People are like stained-glass windows.
They sparkle and shine when the sun is out,
but when the darkness sets in;
their true beauty is revealed,
only if there is a light from within."
-Elizabeth Kübler-Ross

"To be truly involved in life is to be prophetic. To be a
prophet without experiencing the pain of rejection, failure,
and being misunderstood is impossible."
—Robert Wicks, Reflections: Psychological and Spiritual
Images of the Heart

Feeling a Feeling

K eith and Kerri were newlyweds. One evening Kerri was storming around the apartment while Keith tried to watch his favorite baseball team on T.V. Kerri became increasingly agitated and began making noise by slamming things on the counter and on the table around the area Keith was sitting. At first Keith didn't notice as he was absorbed in the game, but as the noise became louder he inquired, "Kerri, What's wrong?" To which Kerri responded, "Nothing, I'm fine." Clearly she was not fine although Keith did not know what to do or say. Kerri finally settled onto the coach next to Keith and grabbed an apple eating away at it angrily. Keith tried to lighten up the tension by saying "Sheesh, I'm sure glad I'm not that apple." Then Kerri burst into tears and began to cry uncontrollably. Keith was desperately trying to get out of her what was wrong. Finally Kerri responded, "I don't know!" Completely perplexed, Keith asked, "How can you be crying so hysterically and not know why?" To which Kerri responded, "I'm just feeling a feeling." Keith turned off the T.V and looked at Kerri, "Honey, what can I do to help?" Kerri didn't know. She needed to cry and Keith gave her permission to do so. When she felt ready she asked him to hold her and that's exactly what he did.

"I'm just feeling a feeling"

We live in a culture that doesn't like to feel. There are a lot of pain medicines on the market, a lot of drinking establishments, and an increase in eating disorder patients at earlier and earlier ages, thus it truly is an accomplishment to just be able to feel our feelings. Even if we don't always understand our feelings, sometimes it helps just knowing it is okay to have them.

Each of us also has our own unique experience with feelings. Have you ever talked to siblings from the same family, with the same parents, and their account of things differs dramatically? That is because each sibling experienced the family differently; each perceived and felt things differently. Two sisters might have experienced the same event—say, a birthday party for the older sister—but one sister interprets it positively while the other interprets it negatively. To the older sister, it was a joyous occasion, made so by the presence of her many friends and their thoughtful gifts. To the younger sister, it was yet another sign that Mom really likes sister number one better. We cannot base how another feels on how we ourselves feel. We have to acknowledge that our perceptions are unique, and allow each person his or her own feelings.

The reality that we all experience things differently is evidenced in the field of medicine as well. In a study by Reuters Health, it was reported that some doctors dismiss individual complaints during a routine procedure based on data that the majority of people breeze through the procedure. However, research confirms that individuals experience pain differently and doctors should not dismiss individual complaints.

Free to Feel

Heather and her husband, Jim, suffered the loss of a child through miscarriage. Heather shared that many well-meaning people, with the best of intentions, would say things that felt like salt on an open wound. Comments that certainly were not intended to cause harm, but did so nonetheless, such as: "You will have other children," "At least you already have a child," "Thank goodness it happened early in the pregnancy," It is God's will," or "It wasn't meant to be." Heather related that the most comforting response she got was when she saw one of her friends, a loving woman who simply walked up to her, wrapped her arms around her, and hugged her tightly. She never said a word; she didn't have to. Heather was not talked out of her feelings; she was allowed the dignity of having them.

Sometimes relational ministry is a quiet exchange.

In spite of the gift of that loving friend, Heather began to question her own feelings, and felt the need to check them out with her husband, Jim. "What is wrong with me?" she asked. "Why does this hurt so badly? Others who have gone through the same thing seem to handle it so much better. I can't stop crying and grieving? Is it my lack of faith? My lack of trust? My weakness in not being able to deal with the loss of a child?"

Jim sought the Holy Spirit when answering Heather's heartfelt questions. "Heather, you feel things very intensely and with great love, and that is a gift. We just lost our child. People mean well. They care, but they just don't know what to say. Forgive them, and let yourself feel your feelings. You have a right to them."

Heather and Jim also had every reason to feel the way they did and they also had a choice on how to respond. Jim suggested the loving way - with acceptance, dignity, and forgiveness. He could have chosen a different path, one of anger, resentment, and hurtful comments such as "You have no idea what we are going through," "You have it so easy; nothing like this has ever happened to you," or even the self-inflicted pain in comments such as "I deserved this," This is because of my sins," or "God hates me." Heather and Jim didn't have a choice regarding their child's life, but they did have a choice on how they would deal with and respond to their feelings.

Feelings are Involuntary – Actions are not

If we project our feelings on another person we put them on the defensive. If, however, we focus on what changes we can make in ourselves, we avoid hurting others and are able to act in love. We all make choices on how we respond to feelings. When I am angry, I can choose unhealthy choices, such as yelling, provoking an argument, pouting, road raging, ignoring, lashing out, etc., or I can acknowledge the feelings, accept them as my own, and understand that I don't have to act on them. There are also options to help one cope with feelings such as talking to a friend, praying, journaling, exercising and removing oneself from an unhealthy situation. It is important to find an outlet that allows you your feelings without having to respond negatively.

Allowing Feelings

Jane was a volunteer parent at a youth retreat. During an activity one of the teen girls named Trinity, approached Jane and asked if she could talk to her. Jane and Trinity decided to go outside and sit on the porch so they could visit. Trinity began to share that she was having a hard time at home and she really needed someone to talk to. Jane was honored Trinity trusted her and listened intently to what she wanted to share. Trinity said that she often felt lonely and unimportant at home. Her parents had a ministry that cared for foreign exchange students and she felt like they were so busy with those others kids that they did not have time for her. She even admitted feeling guilty for saying or thinking such things, but it was how she felt. Recently she had found herself finding comfort in food just to relieve some of the loneliness, but that was now causing a whole new set of problems. She was really unhappy and needed to be honest with someone. Jane was focused on Trinity, listening intently and did not notice another adult nearby listening to their conversation. Kelli was the other adult who decided to interrupt with some well-meaning advice. "Trinity, I couldn't help but over-hear your conversation. I have to tell you that I know your parents very well and they love you so much. They give so much of their time and energy to others to help teach you about the importance of outreach to others. They sacrifice so they can live out this amazing call that

128

they have. You should be thankful to have such a special family."
No matter how true anything Kelli said, that was the last thing
Trinity needed at that moment. This in no way validated any of her
feelings. What she need was to feel supported, listened to, accepted,
and loved. Fortunately Jane had the wisdom to remove Trinity from
that intervention and the two of them continued their talk on a walk
together. Jane apologized for the intrusion.

How many of us get uncomfortable when someone shares a feeling we don't think they should have? How many times have we tried to talk them out of that feeling? "Don't cry, it will be okay," "I'm sure they didn't mean it that way," "It wasn't that bad. You're just overreacting." None of it is helpful to the person trying to work through their feelings. They only spiral into guilt and shame for having those feelings at all.

Too Old to Cry?

There is a classic band aid commercial where a little girl falls down, scrapes her knee, and begins to cry. She runs to her mom, who is quick to provide the perfect remedy, which in this case, is the advertised plastic strip. The little girl's cut has been bandaged and she runs off as good as new.

The little girl was hurt and she sought comfort in her mother's touch. She ran to someone whom she trusted, whom she knew she could count on. She was able to freely shed tears and express her needs, just as children do. Before, that is, they are told they're too old to cry.

When does our thinking change and we grow into the mistaken belief that we are too old to cry? Or even to ask for help? When do we decide that it is weak to seek others' assistance or admit that we need help?

We all know how difficult it can be to get in touch with hurts, and we also know that not everything is healed with a band aid, although we would like to believe so sometimes. We also know that the pains of a relational wound are much more difficult to heal. Unfortunately, we have yet to find an adequate bandage for a broken heart.

Dr. Coghill sites in his medical study that we do in fact assimilate pain differently, and we believe that includes the synergistic relationships that takes place among the physical, spiritual, and emotional domains. Even Jim and Heather experienced the loss of the same child differently. While Heather talked about her feelings to friends and opened up to her husband, Jim retreated to work, held his feelings in, and kept as busy as possible with business-related tasks. Heather used the tools of relational ministry to help her cope with her loss, even if Jim chose to keep his feelings to himself.

We will all know pain and suffering, but as we become more proficient in expressing our feelings we realize we do not have to bear our burdens alone.

Feelings are not indicators of our moral worth; they come to us largely unbidden, sneaking up on us. We can get overwhelmed causing them to spiral deeper inward instead of reaching out, and sharing our feelings with another. Feelings are messengers, inviting us to grow into deeper consciousness and awareness. Some people joke they are overfeelers. Many of us can relate, but that can be a good thing too!

Grace-Filled Grief

Kim, a fitness professional, is a woman of deep spirituality. She exudes a charismatic energy with her positive attitude and kind heart.

Kim often talked about her desire to have more children, and was honest in sharing the pain she and her husband experienced after several miscarriages. When Kim learned that she was once again pregnant, those at the fitness club where she worked were ecstatic.

Kim took it easy her last trimester, taking a break from teaching. Although everyone missed her, they were proud of her for listening to her body and slowing down, something most exercise enthusiasts struggle doing. Everyone was anxiously awaiting the exciting news of

*whether Kim would have a boy or a girl as her due date approached.
But when the call finally came, no one was prepared for the news Kim
would deliver; their newborn baby girl had died during the delivery.
"Her name is Julia," Kim said when she called. "Can you let everyone know?"*

*After such a tragic loss, many expected Kim to question God.
"Why, God? How could you let this happen?" However, Kim never
questioned, instead she channeled all her energy and grief into her
faith. She would tell people "Hopefully we can help others through
our own grief filled experience." Kim's response to her own tragedy
had a huge impact on others.*

Expressing our Feelings

There is no appropriate time to hurt others with our feelings. Some people try to defend their hurtful attacks or comments as "I am just forthright", "I am truthful", "I am assertive",
or "I am direct". We are not denying anyone those qualities,
but they cannot be used as an excuse to hurt another person.
Others say "Well, that is just the way I am, "That is the way I
have always been", or "That is just my personality". That too is
just an excuse. We are all called to take responsibility for our
actions and if what we have always been is causing other's
harm, then we need to change.

"I'm Enough... because God's love is Enough"

Many of us struggle with self forgiveness. The idea that
we are enough is a hard concept to accept. We build our case
against ourselves throughout life. We want to please our parents, teachers, friends, spouses, and children. We constantly
struggle in our quest to measure up to others' expectations.
God is the only one who can fill us in this way. Yet we continue to seek outside approval. So how then are we to filter out
the negative messages of the world and allow our hearts to be
filled with the messages of God? Messengers that tell us: "You
are my beloved child, with whom I am well pleased", "You are

holy and wonderfully made", "I made you with a specific purpose and created you for amazing things", "You are adored, and loved exactly as you are, perfect in my sight".

Many of us have a hurt somewhere within. Have you ever tried to keep a beach ball under water without letting it be seen or even emerge to the surface? From time to time it pops up until you try to stuff it down again, each time lowering it, and adding force so it will not come up again. Yet in time, you grow weary, and the ball rides up again. It is only is a matter of time until it is fully exposed. The same is true for our feelings. When we try to run, hide or stuff them, they keep coming up.

> "If we don't deal with our feelings, they will deal with us."

Handwritten sign found on Mother Teresa's Wall

People are unreasonable, illogical, and self-centered;
Forgive them anyway.

If you are kind, people may accuse you of selfish, ulterior
motives; Be kind anyway.

If you are successful, you will win some false friends, &
some true enemies;
Be successful anyway.

If you are honest and frank, people may cheat you;
Be honest and frank anyway.

What you spend years building, someone could destroy
overnight; Build anyway.

If you find serenity and happiness, others may be jealous;
Be happy anyway.

The good you do today, people will often forget
tomorrow;
Do good anyway.

Give the world the best you have, and it may never be
enough;
Give the world your best anyway.

In the final analysis, it is between you and God.
It was never between you and them anyway.

Questions for Personal Reflection and Discussion

1. How have you dealt with suffering in your life?
2. Do you know someone who has dealt with grief in extraordinary ways?
3. How do you usually express your feelings?
4. What is one specific thing you would like to work on regarding communicating your feelings?
5. Do you have a support system in place when difficult times occur? If not how can you go about building one?
6. Who could you talk to about your feelings?

Chapter Twelve
Wash Each Other's Feet with Forgiveness

"Forgive us our trespasses as we forgive those who trespass against us."
-Matthew 6:14, 15

"Therefore if you bring your gift to the altar, and there remember that your brother has something against you, leave your gift there before the altar, and go your way. First be reconciled to your brother, and then come and offer your gift."
-Mt 5:23-24

"Stay on good terms with each other, held together by love."
- Hebrews 13:1

Pain Management

G iven the hurt and pain that we experience in our relational struggles, is it any wonder that there are so many pain relievers on the market?

There is a remedy for our relational pain and that is healing and forgiveness. It is always accessible, but not always accessed. The healing sanctuary is our heart, and the key to opening it is forgiveness. As Robert DeGrandis, Catholic priest and author, writes, "Forgiveness is an act of the will, not a feeling. It is a lifelong obligation. Daily we need to forgive those who hurt or injure us."

"Forgiveness is an act of the will, not a feeling. It is a lifelong obligation. Daily we need to forgive those who hurt or injure us." Fr. Robert DeGrandis

---

How to Pray

"Our Father in heaven, hallowed be your name. Your kingdom come, your will be done, on earth as in heaven. Give us today our daily bread; and forgive us our debts, as we forgive our debtors; and do not subject us to the final test, but deliver us from the evil one. If you forgive others their transgressions, your heavenly Father will forgive you." (Mt 6:9-14)

In "The Lord's Prayer," we ask God to forgive us as we forgive others. But do we really believe God will forgive us? Do we really believe that no matter what we do, God will welcome us into his arms?

A Father's Forgiveness

A man had two sons, and the younger son said to his father, 'Father, give me the share of your estate that should come to me.' So the father divided the property between them. After a few days, the younger son collected all his belongings and set off to a distant country where he squandered his inheritance on everything, a severe famine struck that country and he found himself in dire need. Coming to his senses, he got up and went back to his father. While he was still a long way off, his father caught sight of him, and was filled with compassion. He ran to his son, embraced him and kissed him. His son said to him, 'Father, I have sinned against heaven and against you; I no longer deserve to be called your son.' But his father ordered his servants; 'Quickly bring the finest robe and put it on him; put a ring on his finger and sandals on his feet. Take the fattened calf and slaughter it. Then let us celebrate with a feast, because this son of mine wad dead, and has come back to life again; he was lost, and has been found.' (Lk 15: 11-14; 17-24a)

The father of the Prodigal Son forgives what others seem to think is unforgivable. He does not give him a condition by which he will accept him back or tell him about his wrong choices and how it affected the family. He only runs to him, embraces him and welcomes him with open arms. Are we this loving in our own relationships? Or do we turn away from the healing power of God's love? Do we reject the presence of a loving, forgiving God?

Pain produces perseverance, strength, growth, and can even produce a conversion experience. The healthiest response to pain, both physical and spiritual, might be: What have I learned? How has this experience helped me grow?

Our most powerful stories are usually the most painful ones. Whether it's losing a job, experiencing a divorce, or being diagnosed with cancer, we have the potential to not only survive but to thrive. As always, Jesus is our model. He endured lies, betrayal, revenge, power struggles, jealousy, arrogance, ego, false conviction, scourging, injustice, suffering, unfathomable pain, and execution. However, rather than leaving us despondent, he offers us new hope, resurrection and new life.

What cross or trial are you facing today? What value do you see in that cross? Where do you see God's presence in it?

Responding to Injustice with Forgiveness

> "Father, forgive them; for they know not what they do." (Lk 23:34)

On April 19, 1995, at 9:02 a.m., Bud Welch's life changed forever when his only child, Julie, was killed in the Murrah Federal Building bombing in Oklahoma City. "The pain following her death was nearly unbearable, and I was consumed with rage and a desire for revenge," Bud recalls. "I wanted an immediate execution for Tim McVeigh, and I believed I could have done it with my bare hands. In time, however, I began to realize that my rage was getting me no where, and eventually it became clear that executing Tim McVeigh would not help emotionally. It would not bring Julie back."

Since that time, Bud has testified before national and world leaders opposing the death penalty, recalling Julie's own words, spoken long ago, that all the death penalty accomplishes is to "teach children to hate."

One of the healing steps Bud needed to take was to visit Timothy McVeigh's family. "I sat in the kitchen where this boy grew up and talked with his father and his sister," he recalls. "I saw a picture on the wall of the man who had masterminded the brutal killing of my only child along with 167 other daughters, sons, sisters, brothers, mothers, fathers, aunts, uncles, and grandchildren. I saw my daughter's killer in a portrait hung on the wall, a photograph of a father's beloved child. I sat with this family and I experienced their grief. I saw things from a bigger paradigm than just my own. They were suffering as well, in a way even I could not fathom. Together we cried. That day I offered forgiveness to them, and to their son, and I vowed to do whatever I could to keep them from experiencing what I was going through."

Bud became a vocal opponent of the death penalty, commenting that Tim McVeigh's execution "did not bring back my daughter, and now another family is planning a funeral for their child. I truly believed it would bring me healing and closure, but the truth is I didn't feel any of those things. It didn't bring the comfort I had hoped for."

Bud knows that true healing starts in the heart. It starts with forgiveness.

Turning Loss into Life

Rose and Mark are a beautiful couple who have always been active in their community and are deeply loved by all. The couple was blessed with two children, Jennifer and Steven. Jennifer was a young teen and Steven her enamored little brother. During a routine doctor's appointment, it was discovered that Jennifer's body was infiltrated with cancer. "Aggressive, incurable, and spreading rapidly" were the horrifying words the doctors spoke to Rose and Mark, whose world would never be the same again.

News spread rapidly throughout their small community, and support came in waves. Cards, visits, phone calls, fundraising dances, and prayer services were the response of their many friends and acquaintances. For Jennifer, there were long nights in hospitals, experimental treatments, and vicious spells of nausea, fatigue, and pain. And for Mark, Rose, and Steven, the agonizing torture of helplessly watching their daughter and sister suffer.

Rose and Mark's response to their daughter's disease amazed the community who loved them. They acted in faith, hope and love. Even during the most trying moments, there was a peace about them. They did not deny their pain, but instead embraced and accepted it, and, in time, would ask themselves what they had learned from it.

As a result of Jennifer's illness and death, the community came together like never before. They knew firsthand the fragility of life. Jennifer reminded everyone of how precious each moment is, how precious each life is, how precious each person is.

"It's only when we truly know and understand that we have a limited time on earth—and that we have no way of knowing when our time is up—that we will begin to live each day to the fullest, as if it was the only one we had." - Elisabeth Kubler-Ross

---

We are told that there is a significantly higher divorce rate for couples who have lost a child. Many are not able to overcome the tremendous sense of loss. Their grief is turned first inward and then outward against the other.

"Death is not the greatest loss in life. The greatest loss is what dies inside us while we live," writes Norman Cousins.

Mark and Rose focused on one another and Steven. Much to everyone's surprise, especially Mark, Rose and Steven's – the couple became pregnant again and gave birth to a beautiful baby boy. That in itself would be a beautiful example of the new life that the couple experienced as they came together in their suffering, but God was not done with them yet. Shortly after their new son was born, Rose and Mark were pregnant again with another boy. They embraced their precious gifts and knew that their special angel in heaven would be smiling down on this household of boys, protecting them as only a big sister could. Long after Jenny's death, Mark and Rose continued as beacons of light to their community, reaching out to those in need with compassion. They understand and have walked through the valley of darkness in watching their child suffer and die. They now walk with others, comforting them through their trials and helping them believe in the hope of new life.

How we cope with the pain of loss and grief involves many things, including our attitude, support systems, resources, experiences, and emotional state.

There are so many ways to deal with pain in our lives. Many spiral downward, build up walls, harbor resentments, close doors, or just shut down. But when we let God hold us, we can reach out to others and use our own experience to help someone else.

When Jesus washed the disciples' feet, he was not only removing external dirt from their body, he was also purifying their heart. When we face unbearable hurt, pain, loneliness, and loss, Jesus is there, ready to hold us. Draw near to him; he is waiting.

Healing the Hurt

(Fr. Gale Shares)

A woman came to my office who had been sexually abused by her father while she was a young child. "I hate him!" she said, "but he is dying of cancer and I need to go see him. I feel as though I can't go. There is such hatred and bitterness in my heart that I can't resolve this."

She had written a letter to him describing the pain that she had suffered from his actions and asked if she could read it to me. It took her a full forty-five minutes to read it; it was so painful to feel and relive those feelings.

When she finished, I knelt down before her and metaphorically taking the place of her father, asked her for forgiveness. It took her another forty-five minutes to actually say the words, "Yes, I forgive you." When she finally spoke the words, she sobbed and held me, still kneeling, in the tightest bear hug imaginable for the longest time. I had cramps in my legs and knees for a week!

When she returned to see me after the week, she was disappointed. "I was unable to touch him," she explained. So I said to her, "Well, let's pray for the grace of touch then." We did and again finished with a hug. (This time not on my knees- they were still sore!)

After another week, she returned with a smile. "I went to the hospital and leaned on the door," she explained, "and when the time was right, I laid my hands on his ankle and then on his shoulder, and I was able to tell him, 'I love you.'" She had to rid herself of the infection that lingered from the wound that had grown and deepened over the years. That is what forgiveness does—it heals the infection.

Jesus knew how to separate sin from sinner, the person from the infection. He never denied or shut off the relationship; rather, he loved and provided guidance through acceptance, empowering, and at times redirecting.

Family Forgiveness through Prayer

(Fr. Gale Shares)

I am the oldest of six children. My father would say that I was the first and the worst. As adults, we all lived as far away from each other as possible until my brother Leo moved to a nearby city with his family. I am a very busy priest, so I would only see him every two years or so. My mother was always saying, "When are you going to see Leo?" So one Sunday afternoon as I finished an Engaged Encounter weekend, I noticed on my calendar that there was nothing scheduled for the remainder of the day, so I decided to go see Leo. In addition, my mom had laid enough guilt on me over the years about not visiting my brother (and I had some of my own), so there was no way out of doing my duty.

At the time, Leo's children were eleven, nine, seven, and four. When I arrived, the kids came running out to the car with shouts of "Uncle Gale is here! Uncle Gale is here!" and that just made me feel even guiltier. As a result of my increasing guilt, I said, "I'm not just stopping by for a quick visit; I'm going to stay for dinner! In fact, I'm going to stay for your night prayers!" In no time, I would be reminded of why I had chosen the life of a celibate priest.

Now, not having children of my own, I can't claim to be an authority on what normal childhood activity is or isn't. But if those kids are normal, God help those parents with abnormal kids. These kids were up the wall and on the ceiling and under the floor. The house was a battlefield. Dinner, which I had voluntarily stayed for, was total chaos. All the while I was thinking, "Oh my, I could be in my rectory by myself, at my own table, with my own newspaper. When I go home tonight, I will schedule something on my calendar every day for the next twenty years so I'm not tempted to do this again."

If I had assumed that a full dinner would result in somewhat more docile children, well, I was in for yet another surprise. They must have eaten something that further energized them for they just got worse. I asked Leo and his wife, Nancy, if it ever ends. The resigned looks on the faces confirmed my worse fears.

Later, when bath time came around, I heard one of the kids screaming that the water was too hot. I thought, "Ah, this is how they do it. This is how parents get the starch out of their kids—they scald them into submission!"

Shortly after their baths, they arrived back in the family room, snug and comfortable in their pajamas, I began to sense that there might be some normalcy to my brother's family after all. With absolutely no prompting, the four children formed a circle with their mom and dad, a circle for prayer.

As Leo began the nightly family prayers, the children's rowdiness abated noticeably. There was still a bit of nudging and giggling, but Leo kept on praying through it. I figured he was trying to impress his brother the priest as he maintained a steady pace of familiar Catholic prayers. As this lingered on for ten minutes, twenty minutes, I began thinking "Leo, even God gets tired, would you just hurry up and be done with it, so I can bolt to the door and leave?" But I was not going to be the first one to break the prayer circle. I'm quite sure one of those unruly kids will do it soon.

Then, just as I am thinking he has finally run out of prayers because he has taken a long breath and I am thanking God to myself, the room got very still and quiet. Leo looked up to Beth, the oldest, and asked, "Do you want to start?" She said, "Yes, Daddy, I will," and she

looked up at Leo and inquired, "Have I hurt you in any way today?"
She went around the room and asked each person the same.

Catherine, the four-year-old, could hardly wait her turn, and in
response to the eagerly anticipated question she responded, "No way,
José," which I subsequently learned was her response every night. If
Leo hadn't asked, she would have been hurt. She is no less important
because of her size; hurt happens at every age.

As Leo continued around the room with no one acknowledging
any hurt, I'm beginning to think, so this is just a ritual and there is
no meaning to it. Just then it comes to Chris, the oldest boy, and he
is going around the room, gets to his mom and asks as quickly as he
can—suspiciously quickly, in fact— "Have I hurt you in any way
today?" Mothers know more about hurt than the rest of us, and she
responded, "Yes, Chris, you have."

My heart almost stopped as I wondered what he could have done
that was worse than any other of them did all afternoon. I thought all
kinds of stuff going on that day that would have qualified as hurts, but
I guess most of that was just the bumps and bruises of normal living.
Yet somehow this little boy crossed the line.

Now, Nancy is one of the most kind, compassionate, tender, and
loving people in this world. She had to say yes, because she had a hurt,
and as she said yes, tears were streaming down my face. I looked up
and everyone else in the room was crying. Chris said, "Please tell me
the hurt." Sensitive as always, Nancy leaned over and told Chris in
his ear, so as to keep the details from the rest of us. But we all heard
Chris ask, "Will you forgive me for this hurt?" As Nancy gave her
forgiveness, the two of them embraced.

"So every time I get in my car and go somewhere I expect
You to be, I never find You, and then when I think You
couldn't possibly be in such an ordinary place, there You
are. You've done it again."

As I drove away that evening, I thought to myself, "okay, okay,
so every time I get in my car and go somewhere I expect You to be,

I never find You, and then when I think You couldn't possibly be in such an ordinary place, there You are. You've done it again."

That's been the truth. I have never been to a more sacred place than one in which two people who have a broken relationship through hurt, heal each other through the power of forgiveness. Leo and Nancy told me that about a month after this episode they were on their way to an important church event. They were running out the door and told the kids that they would have to say night prayer by themselves. The kids responded, "You mean we won't be able to forgive each other tonight?" They know!

(Fr. Gale's brother Leo recently passed away. Our deepest sympathy and prayers are with Fr. Gale and his family.)

Healing in our Churches

There are those who have experienced preachers and religious life attempting to use shame-based preaching to influence.

The particular tragedy of shame-based pastoral approaches is that it affects so many people negatively. Many put such faith in the preacher that they feel that person is speaking for God. If the preacher condemns, then it is God who is condemning, and the congregation is introduced to a paradigm of God that is narrow and exclusive. This paradigm of God then becomes the paradigm for the congregants' many interpersonal relationships, creating a cycle of exclusivity, us versus them-ism, guilt, and anxiety.

During the past decade, many churches, some of which we have had direct experience with, have endured scandal, hurt, and excruciating mistrust. How can a wound so deep, so far-reaching, be healed? Where do we start?

Healing our Church Family

A youth minister named Glenn worked in a rural church that had a school. Being a naturally loving and embracing man, he wondered if he would ever be able to hug a young person again, given the "safe environment" changes taking place in his church in response to the clergy sex abuse scandal.

These thoughts consumed him, and he found himself questioning his call to ministry at such an awkward and painful time in the church. Not only did he wonder how the ripple effect would influence his position as youth minister, but how it would affect others as well. Holy men who were once thought of in high regard were now feared, and the very cloth they wore as a symbol of their commitment to holiness was now seen as a sign of danger.

One afternoon, Glenn was walking through the church school, heavy-hearted after a long meeting about all the new rules and sanctions being implemented to protect the innocent. Glenn, always an advocate for safety, was concerned that some members were over reacting in fear, and the rigidity of rules and regulations would stifle relationships with the youth, restrictions like not being able to greet someone with the usual hug. Glenn knew there was healing power in touch and he was concerned about what might be lost in this swing of the pendulum.

While deep in thought about these issues, Glenn caught a sudden movement out of the corner of his eye. It was Fr. Fred, the pastor, playfully poking his head in and out of one of the classrooms. Fr. Fred would pop his head in the classroom and the children would giggle, and just as the teacher would glance up to see what was causing the laughter, he would duck back out. As soon as the teacher got the students quieted down, the game would start up again, with Fr. Fred peeking in and making his faces and the children responding with squeals of delight. Finally, the teacher caught on and called out into the hallway, "Fr. Fred would you like to join us?" With that invitation, he was in the door.

Glenn watched closely as Fr. Fred entered the room and several children spontaneously got up from their chairs and came over to hug him. Without thinking or hesitating, Fr. Fred kneeled down on his aged knees to be at eye level with the children. Images of "Let the children come to Me." came to Glenn's mind.

"Then children were brought to him that he might lay his hands on them and pray. The disciples rebuked them, but Jesus said, "Let the children come to me, and do not prevent them; for the kingdom of heaven belongs to such as these. "After he placed his hands on them, he went away". (Mt. 19:13-15)

Soon they had all gathered around him, talking and hugging, the teacher smiling at the interruption.

Glenn continued to observe all this unnoticed. At one point he could barely see Fr. Fred's head among all the children circled together around him. At that moment, Glenn smiled with the visual of Fr. Fred's gentle touch and he was reminded that there is always hope for a hurting world, and it starts with one person loving another, and another, and ...

God gives us the pure in heart, the children, to remind us when we forget. They are always willing to forgive, willing to forget, and ready to leap with love. It is also our important responsibility to ask for forgiveness. Fr. Fred had extended that plea for forgiveness to his congregation who were deeply hurting. What he found was that people are very forgiving when given the opportunity or when asked for forgiveness. Sometimes what is most needed is the hurt to simply be acknowledged.

"I'm sorry for your hurt."

(Fr. Gale Shares)

I got called one day by a dear friend, Samantha. Her father was in the hospital dying. She pleaded, "Will you go see my dad? He hasn't been to church in 30 years and has resisted all visits by the hospital clergy. Maybe you can help him!" Knowing how much it would mean to Samantha, I agreed to her request.

After the initial pleasantries, I jumped right in: "So I hear you have a hurt with the church. Do you want to talk about it?"

The dying man sharply retorted, "No, I don't have a hurt. Christians are all just a bunch of sorry SOB's and I have no use for them."

I immediately recognized the deep hurt the man was carrying and responded with love: "Can you tell me about it? What happened?"

The man had never told anyone about his hurt. Instead, he had stormed off mad 30 years ago and never looked back. Ironically, it's usually the little things that we let fester for years.

He let me pray with him. I knelt down beside him and said, "On behalf of all his brothers and sisters in the church, I am humbly sorry for what the church has done. Will you forgive me as a member of the church that hurt you?" The man granted forgiveness and Samantha told me he died later that night in peace.

Relationship Amnesia

We've all been encouraged to forgive and forget; words that are much easier to say than do. Many have adopted the "I forgive you but I will never forget" attitude. Relational ministry uses Jesus' model of forgiveness '70 x 7'.

"Then came Peter to him, and said, Lord, how often shall my brother sin against me, and I forgive him? Seven times?" Jesus replied, "I say not seven times, but seventy times seven." (Matthew 18.21)

There is an entire constellation of reasons why the Lord chose the '70 x 7' model which represents the perfection and completeness of forgiveness.

This does not however require relationship amnesia. It is imperative that we learn from our relationship mistakes and not move back into harmful or destructive relational patterns. Forgetting does not imply a loss of memory; instead it provides the healing opportunity to put a hurt behind and allows us to move forward without forgetting the lesson.

The following is a three-step process that helps in all situations, especially when we are trying to understand and learn from our relationships.

3 Key Questions:

1. What happened? As you explore what happened in the relationship, you will be able to understand the situation and gain perspective. Then you can work to identify what your part was and what you are capable of changing.

2. What did I learn? As you invite this question, you find out not only what you learned about another person but what you learned about yourself—the things that are important to you, who you are, how you handled things, and what brought that about.

3. What can I do differently next time? As we move to the third question, we are able to release ourselves with forgiveness. If we learned a painful lesson, we can be strengthened by the experience. We can create a plan of action and be empowered with the wisdom to do things differently next time. It is always better to be accountable than to be a victim. We have the power to make our own choices and the responsibility to ask for forgiveness for our poor ones. If there are amends that need to be made, now is the time to work toward restitution.

"I release you with love. You did the best you could with who you are and what you knew, and I forgive you."

When these three steps have been worked through, close with the statement "I release you with love. You did the best you could with who you are and what you knew, and I forgive you." You may even need to include yourself in this forgiveness exercise.

Forgiveness requires action. The second part of the word 'for-give' is the action verb 'give'. Forgiveness not only takes place in our mind; it takes place through our actions. Resentment immobilizes while forgiveness empowers.

If someone is toxic to our spirit, we don't have to be around them. Though everyone is important to God, not everyone has to be in our direct circle of influence. We can love someone from afar. We are called to love everyone. We are called to relationally minister to everyone. We are not called to be *in relationship* with everyone.

One of our wounded beliefs is that we're not good enough, certainly not good enough to be forgiven. For some reason, it is so much easier for us to accept that others are worthy of God's unconditional love and forgiveness even when we feel we are not. If you struggle with self-forgiveness, know that you are not alone. The idea that we are forgiven is a difficult one to accept. We constantly struggle in our quest to measure up to others' expectations, forgetting that we are made in the image of God and that upon making us, "He saw that it was good."

Accepting the unconditional love of God drowns out those negative messages allowing us to heal. He has forgiven you; go now and forgive yourself.

"You have already been forgiven"

Hannah was praying outside an abortion clinic, offering counsel to the women going in. She had counseled many women over the years that had abortions and told her that they wished she was at the clinic the day they went in. Maybe they would not have gone through with it. They encouraged her to keep reaching out to hurting women in unplanned pregnancies and that there was no way anyone could ever know about the post trauma after an abortion. Hannah knew how scared these women were and she wanted to help in anyway she could.

She was reflecting in prayer when a tall, slender woman emerged from the clinic. The woman's hands were tightly clenched across her barren stomach. She looked so fragile; Hannah wished she could hold her up. Noticing the tears on her cheeks, Hannah gently whispered to the woman as she drew near, "Jesus loves you." The woman whose tears were now streams looked up at Hannah and said, "I wish I could believe you, but I am a Christian. I know God will never forgive me for this." Hannah, familiar with that lie, responded again, "Precious

151

sister in Christ, He already has; it has been done, you are forgiven."
She then gave the woman some literature on post-abortion counseling
and shared her own number.

We are all broken, but God never gives up on us. It is a lie that God's own children would be unworthy of his love. We don't get to decide his love for us; we can only choose whether or not we will accept that love—and whether or not we return it.

What we believe about ourselves is our choice, too. The Bible tells us that God looks upon our heart. He knows our suffering and he suffers with us. Letting God love us when we suffer and when we feel unlovable is one way we begin to heal our spirit.

When we believe lies such as 'we are worthless failures incapable of making good decisions', than we are more likely to live out those messages through self-fulfilling prophecy. When we see ourselves made in God's image and likeness, forgiven and loved, we are more likely to reflect back our innate goodness in our actions. How we feel about ourselves and how we accept God's love for us will be translated in our relationships.

A lesson in forgiveness from Adam and Eve

Forgiveness is necessary for true healing to transpire. Looking at the first couple, Adam and Eve we wonder what might have happened if they had handled their imperfections differently and forgiven themselves and each another. What if Adam and Eve could have embraced the forgiveness of God instead of running? Did God say, "You are naked; now get out of here and hide?" No, God obviously did not say that, but Adam and Eve did hide. Whether we see this story as literal or metaphorical, the truth remains that we all have the choice to distance ourselves from God or to turn to him even when we mess up.

Who were Adam and Eve hiding from? God? Have you ever tried to hide from God? It doesn't work. It didn't work for Adam and Eve, it didn't work for Jonah, and it doesn't work for us. Adam and Eve saw their own weakness, their own sin, and they thought themselves unworthy. But God never stopped loving them, nor does he stop loving us.

Let's invite Adam and Eve to experience reconciliation and forgiveness. Yes, God knows our sin; he knows our weakness, and guess what? He loves us anyway. God forgives us. There is nothing we can do to make him stop being madly in love with us!

The problem is that the very concept of God's unwavering love for us is almost unfathomable. We don't know how to love unconditionally, so we struggle with the idea of being loved that way. We put our own human limits on God, even to his infinite love. We create an image of God based on human understanding, and what we understand is judgmentalism, criticism, fault-finding, and limitations. God has no limits.

What if we can grow to accept God's love for us on God's terms? What would it look like? We imagine it would look like: joy, peace, patience, kindness, forgiveness, healing, and, ultimately, a loving world. Acceptance of God's love is our first step in loving our neighbor and ourselves in just the way God calls us to.

Take a moment to bask in God's love for you, wrap yourself in his warm blanket of forgiveness, and allow him to heal you as only he can. One exercise is to write down all the things keeping you from experiencing God's love in its totality. Then let it go burn it if that helps, share it with someone if you want to and release it. Let anything that stands between you and God go. Once you forgive yourself, it will be much easier to forgive others.

Healing: Mind, Body, and Spirit

> "Anyone can be a heart specialist.
> All you have to do is love someone."

In a recent medical study, people who generally had forgiving natures tended to have lower blood pressure compared to people who were not as forgiving. Since chronic high blood pressure is a risk factor for stroke and other serious health ailments, we can assist our physical health by dealing with our emotional health, just by letting bygones be bygones.

How can the simple act of forgiving affect us physically? Think about it: Have you ever felt depressed and responded by overeating? Or had headaches, stomach aches, dizziness, fatigue, or exhaustion as a result of a relationship stress? Our emotions strongly impact our physiology. When we harbor resentment, anger, and unforgiveness, our bodies tend to respond in unforgiving ways toward us, providing us with a message that something is askew in our lives.

Forgiveness is good for us! It is good for the giver and the receiver. It is good for our spiritual condition, our emotional well being and our physical wellness.

Go now and Wash Each Other's Feet with Forgiveness...

Forgiveness Prayer:
By Fr. Robert DeGrandis-modified-05

Lord Jesus Christ, I ask today that I may forgive everyone in my life. I know that You will give me strength to forgive and I thank You that You love me more than I love myself and want my happiness more than I desire it for myself.

Lord, I forgive **myself** for my sins, faults and failings. For all that is truly bad in myself or all that I think is bad, I do forgive myself. For any delvings into the occult, and any idol worship, I forgive myself. Also for taking Your name in vain, for not worshipping You; for hurting my parents; for getting drunk; for taking drugs; for sins against my purity; for adultery; for abortion; for stealing; for lying; I am truly forgiving myself today. Thank you, Lord, for your grace at this moment.

I truly forgive **my mother**. I forgive her for all the times she hurt me, resented me, was angry with me and for all the times she punished me. I forgive her for the times she preferred my brothers or sisters over me. I forgive her for the times she told me I was dumb, ugly, stupid, the worst of the children, or that I cost the family a lot of money. Also for the times she told me I was unwanted, an accident, a mistake or not what she expected, I forgive her.

I forgive **my father**. I forgive him for any non-support any lack of love, affection or attention. I forgive him for any lack of time, for not giving me his companionship, for his drinking, for arguing and fighting with my mother, and the children. For his severe punishments, for desertion, for being away from home, for working too much, for divorcing my mother or for any running around, I do forgive him.

Lord, I extend forgiveness to **my sisters** and **brothers**. I forgive those who rejected me, lied about me, hated me, resented me, competed for my parents' love; those who hurt me or physically harmed me. For those who were too severe on me, punished me or made my life unpleasant in anyway, I do forgive them.

155

Lord, I forgive **my spouse** *for any lack of love, affection, consideration, support, attention, communication; for faults, failings, weaknesses, and those other acts or words that hurt or disturb me.*

Jesus, I forgive **my children** *for their lack of respect, obedience, love, attention, support, warmth, understanding; their bad habits, falling away from the church, any bad actions which disturb me.*

My God, I forgive **my son or daughter-in-law and other relatives by marriage,** *who treat my child with a lack of love. For all their words, thoughts, actions or omissions which injure and cause pain, I forgive them.*

Please help me to forgive **my relatives,** *who may have interfered in our family, been possessive, who may have caused confusion or turned one family member against another.*

Jesus, help me to forgive my **co-workers** *who are disagreeable or make life miserable for me. For those who push their work off on me, gossip about me, won't cooperate with me, try to take my job, I do forgive them.*

My **neighbors** *need to be forgiven, Lord. For all their noise, letting their property run down, not tying up their dogs that run through my yard, not taking in their trash barrels, being prejudiced and running down the neighborhood. I do forgive them.*

I forgive my **clergyman,** *my* **congregation** *and my* **church** *for all their lack of support, pettiness, lack of friendliness, not affirming me as they should, not providing me with inspiration, for not using me in a key position, for other hurt they have inflicted, I do forgive them today.*

Lord, I forgive all **professional people** *who have hurt me in any way: doctors, nurses, hospital workers, policemen, lawyers, judges for anything they did to me, I truly forgive them today.*

Lord, I forgive **my employer** *for not paying me enough money, for not appreciating my work, for being unkind and unreasonable with me, for being angry or unfriendly, for not promoting me, and for not complimenting me on my work, for not using my gifts to their full potential.*

Lord, I forgive **my school teachers and instructors** *of the past as well as the present. For those who punished me, humiliated me, in-*

sulted me, treated me unjustly, made fun of me, used derogatory nick names, didn't accept me or encourage me or teach me.

Lord, I forgive my **friends** who have let me down, lost contact with me, do not support me, were not available when I needed help, borrowed money and did not return it, gossiped about me, betrayed me.

Lord Jesus, I especially pray for the grace of forgiveness for that **one person** in life who has **hurt me the most**. I ask to forgive anyone whom I consider my greatest enemy; the one who is the hardest to forgive or the one whom I said I will never forgive.

Thank You, Jesus, that I am free of the evil of unforgiveness. Let Your Holy Spirit fill me with light and let every dark area of my mind be enlightened. Amen

Opportunities for Personal Reflection and Discussion

1. Is there someone you need to forgive today?

2. Is there something you need to forgive yourself for?

3. Is there anyone you could reach out to today that might need to hear from you?

4. Is there a resentment you need to let go of?

5. Do you realize you are enough?

6. Have you forgiven yourself?

7. What hurt are you holding onto today that you need to let go of?

8. What action can you take to achieve healing and forgiveness?

9. Who can you reach out to today?

CONCLUSION
WASHING EACH OTHER'S FEET THROUGH RELATIONAL MINISTRY

"Heart- shattered lives ready for love don't for a moment escape God's notice."
- Psalm 51:17

"Naïve grace is the kind of love that wants everyone to be included instead of finding ways to exclude. Jesus Christ was naïve enough to love anyone and everyone."
—Mike Yaconelli, Dangerous Wonder

"Do you want to see God's infallible plan unfolding before you in the universe right now? His mightiest miracle, His incomparable majesty? His unfathomable mystery? Ready? Behold a miracle... Got a mirror?"

Looking for Nemo and Finding Jesus

Sydney, a youth leader, was thrilled when she was invited to help chaperone teens attending a youth conference. Sydney loves teens and knows they often remind adults to have fun, and to seek more fully the qualities of life that we tend to forget as we mature. She embraced the opportunity to experience once again the gift of these young people who are so full of life and love. Syd went knowing it was she, who would be blessed, but she had no idea that the blessing would come through a deeply painful experience.

The conference theme was based on the popular movie at the time,"Finding Nemo," which the group watched on the bus en route to the conference. The movie is about a father's steadfast pursuit for his lost child, who has run away and it pulls on the heart strings of audiences of all ages.

Focusing on the symbolism of water in the movie, the eloquent keynote speaker, Bob, brought to life images of "fishers of men," "the river of life," "navigating the waters," and "Washing Each Other's Feet." Sydney felt the powerful images of the weekend's theme unfold around her. She enjoyed the positive energy of the conference and the opportunity to connect with the youth, but was oblivious to the negativity surfacing around her. So much so that it would soon change the course of the conference in an entirely different direction for her.

As Sydney was walking with her group of teens to the closing spiritual celebration, she was informed of a discussion that had taken place during the course of the weekend - a discussion about her. She was confused why someone would say something about her without *talking to her? She could not image what she might have done? Feeling hurt and betrayal, she was overwhelmed with emotion. A close friend, noticing Sydney's watering eyes, escorted her to a private area to talk or rather to listen. In the comfort of her friend, Sydney could no longer control the stream of water now flowing down her cheeks. The theme for the weekend was coming to life from within this time: water flowing in the form of tears, the tumultuous tide being her emotions, rough waters being tough times, and of course there are always images of sharks and piranhas when we are hurt.*

Sydney's mind was reeling with questions. These were supposed to be her peers, fellow ministers, Christians, for goodness sake! "Aren't we called to a higher standard?" She questioned. The teens were acting in good faith, of course; it was the adults who were entertaining negativity.

Sydney's friend listened intently, her own eyes now tearing up with empathy as she experienced the pain her friend was going through. As they held each other, the slow healing process started to take effect. Suddenly they were abruptly interrupted by a fellow minister who instructed them that they needed to take their seats for the service. Overwhelmed with sadness, Sydney could not image how her friend could seem so callous to her pain. Sydney descended deeper into her darkness and with that final dagger, she excused herself to the restroom.

In his quest for Nemo, the father had experienced universal compassion from those he encountered, but Sydney was finding herself more and more alone. The rest of the group settled into their seats for the service leaving the halls painstakingly quiet for her hurting heart.

Sydney wondered how she could be at a church conference with 25,000 people, her extended faith community, and yet she had never felt so alone. Just then there was a break in the silence and Syd heard a soft and gentle voice call out to her: "Honey? Honey? Are you okay?"

Sydney looked up and was greeted by a dark-haired woman with the most gentle eyes she had ever seen. Her kind voice was like respite in the desert. There before her was a woman in a uniform and through her blurry tear filled eyes she could just make out the name embroidered in cursive on the woman's shirt pocket...'Maria'.

The compassionate woman spoke again, "Honey, are you okay?" Sydney knew that standing before her was a messenger from God, reminding her that she is not alone. Stopping what she was doing and looking intently at Sydney, Maria persisted, sincerely concerned, "Honey, can I help you? Do you need anything? What can I do to help you?" The words felt like a warm blanket on a snowy day. Someone had acknowledged her hurt and wanted to reach out and soothe her pain. All Sydney could muster was a sincere but crooked smile, and she thanked Maria, assuring her that she would be okay. She told her how thoughtful it was for her to inquire.

Sydney knew that in that moment she was in the presence of the reflection of Jesus. We are all called to be Christ to one another and that is exactly who Maria was to Sydney in that moment. As Sydney started to walk away, her eyes began to focus through the salty tears and she saw for the first time what Maria had been doing prior to stopping her. Mopping! Here was Maria mopping up water, the symbol of the weekend. The stream of water, now being Syd's tears, was being cleaned up by Maria's kindness. The most powerful messenger that weekend was a humble servant, someone out of the spotlight, doing her work and yet taking the time to listen with her heart; to reach beyond herself and into the heart of another's wounded soul, someone who was in desperate need for a compassionate heart.

Each day we have opportunities to be Jesus to someone. There are times we fail to notice these opportunities because of our own to-do lists. Maria had a to-do list also, but she was able to put that aside when the greater need of relational ministry was before her.

We learn lessons from every experience; both the joyful and the painful and we choose how they will affect us. We even choose if we are going to forgive and return to a place of love.

Daily we make choices on whether we will tear down or build up the Body of Christ – One another. What we cannot choose, however, is how much God loves us. His love is beyond all human understanding. Even when we don't choose him, he continues to choose us. When we can't hear him, he finds ways to speak to us. When we can't see him,

163

he reveals himself to us in the most unlikely of places, like a mainte-nance worker named Maria. When we can't feel him, he wraps us up in the warm embrace of one of his messengers- each other.

In the last part of the movie, once Nemo and his Father have found one another, it is again time for Nemo to go off on his own, and spread his wings. His father who had relentlessly searched for him is again saddened at the thought of losing his son again. He had just found him! Suddenly, without warning, Nemo turns back and dives into his Father's arms where his father is greeted with the most tender embrace he had ever received. Nemo whispers, "I love you, Dad," to which the father replies, "I love you too, Son."

Sydney returned to her group after her encounter with Jesus in the form of Maria, and as she did she closed her eyes, embraced the mo-ment, and said, "I love you, Dad." As she spoke those words, a surge of peace engulfed her heart. It was as if she could now feel God's arms embrace her and the gentle whisper of his voice speaking into her heart saying, "I love you too, Sydney. I love you my child." Sydney began her weekend thinking about Nemo. She walked away Finding Jesus.

We have all probably felt like Sydney at one time or an-other— under attack, unfairly judged, persecuted, and hurt. We also have probably been the one with a stone in hand. We all have moments when we neglect the opportunity to Rela-tional Minister to another. Thank goodness for the healing power of forgiveness!

Sydney was able to reconcile with her friends and it turned out to be a misunderstanding. We will all face such hurts in our journey; things that ultimately make us stronger. Forgive-ness and healing allow us to grow beyond our pain; it sets us free and allows us to love more deeply. Life is not easy. The journey can be confusing and painful, and yet throughout love remains, the unconditional love of our Father.

We cannot escape the painful experiences that come our way. What we can do is reach out to each other. When we go looking for Nemo or a version there of, may we all blessed to have Maria's along the way, and when given the opportunity may we choose to act in love in our own lives. There will be those who "wash our feet" with unconditional love and we are called to do the same. We pray for you as you embark upon your own unique and special relational ministry journey. You are ready!

Go now and wash each other's feet...

Questions for Personal Reflection and Discussion

1. Has there ever been a time in your life when you felt like Sydney? Describe your feelings. What did you learn?

2. When in your life has God revealed his love for you through someone else's love?

3. What can we learn from both of these women, Sydney and Maria that can be applied to our own life?

4. Whose feet can you wash today?

5. How will you respond to the call of relational ministry?

6. As you reflect on the messages in this book, what are some of the insights you have gotten in touch with? How will you apply them in your life?

7. What does "Wash Each Other's Feet" mean to you now?

About the Authors

Tammy Amosson is humbled daily by the incredible and awesome love of God in the midst of her stumbling, inadequacy, and messiness. Tammy is the founder of Spiritual Fitness Ministry through which she presents interactive workshops, presentations, and seminars throughout the country. Tammy's high-energy motivational presence encourages those seeking to live more fully in mind, body, and spirit. She is a Nationally Certified Personal Trainer and Fitness Instructor who specializes in working with those who want to be heart healthy. Be warned—her passion is kickboxing! Tammy is also the founder of *Mission Possible*, a service outreach program, and *Seize the Day*, a support group for families with children with seizure disorders. She is a volunteer for the Epilepsy Foundation. Tammy has a B.S. in Family Sciences, a certificate in Youth Ministry Studies, and a minor in addictive disorders counseling. She is a facilitator for Positive Discipline and is currently getting her master's degree at the University of Dallas Institute of Religious and Pastoral Studies. Tammy and her husband, Brett, have their own trinity of sons, Joshua, Jacob, Luke & one coming soon! Tammy can be reached at amosson1@cox.net or 806-358-2826

Fr. Gale White is a retired priest whose principal ministry has been helping couples, families, and communities build and maintain healthy relationships. He has a master's degree from Regis University in Denver in Adult and Family Ministry and was the diocesan co-director of the Adult and Family Ministry Office of the Diocese of Dallas. Through those ministries, he has helped thousands of couples prepare for marriage, enrich their marriages, and enhance healing for hurting marriages and families. Through his popular and well-attended seminars on Healing Life's Hurts, he has assisted people in learning that by forgiving all those who have injured us (including ourselves); we can be free, no longer having to carry past events or persons as stones around our necks. Fr. Gale is currently retired and living as a member of a family in Dallas.

Printed in the United States
37013LVS00004B/1-135

9 781420 865202